THE *Alchemy*
OF LOVE AND SEX

THE *Alchemy*
OF LOVE AND SEX

Lee Lozowick

HOHM PRESS, PRESCOTT, ARIZONA

ISBN: 0-934252-58-0
Library of Congress Catalog Number: 95-077755

Text Design and Layout:
Kim Johansen, *Black Dog Design Co.*
Cover Design: Kim Johansen

Hohm Press
P.O. Box 2501
Prescott, AZ 86302
(520) 778-9189

DEDICATION

To my Father, Yogi Ramsuratkumar,
Without Whom I am nothing and
with Whom, by the Benediction of
His Regard, I am Nothing. All that
is worthwhile here is His, and
all that is not is fully mine.
Jai Bhagawan Yogi Ramsuratkumar Ki Jai.

ACKNOWLEDGEMENTS

This book is the result of many efforts, but primarily those of Vijaya (VJ) Fedorshak who started this project over three years ago and whose passion for this material and compelling desire to see it shared with others motivated him to sift through thousands of pages of recorded transcripts and listen to hundreds of hours of taped lectures to find Mr. Lee's words on this enigmatic and important subject. With the skillful editorial efforts of his wife, Karuna, the material from which this present book is taken was finally assembled in one place, and with such force as to make it undeniable. The author can only express humble acknowledgement and sincere appreciation for their dedicated efforts.

TABLE OF CONTENTS

FOREWORD

By Georg Feuerstein, Ph.D.
Author of *Sacred Sexuality*

Our Identity transcends the bodymind. This is a well-known truth in those circles that uphold the perennial philosophy. It is, however, a truth that calls for more than intellectual assent or pious affirmation. It is a truth that wants to be realized and lived.

The first step to that bone-and-marrow realization is to acknowledge that we are obstructed beings: There are "knots" within our personality structure that actively prevent us from living authentically and seemingly curtail the fullness of our body- and mind-transcending Identity. That apparent curtailment is our unenlightenment.

Upon enlightenment, when all "knots" are released, the wholeness of our Identity becomes obvious. More than that, we realize
that "our" Identity is the same glorious Identity that sustains
and is the ultimate destiny of all beings and things. This realization brings peace and equanimity. For how can we fear, be
in conflict with, or envy others when, in their essence, they are
not different from us? How can we not be happy?

Most people do not have the slightest inkling of such freedom and happiness. Their lives play themselves out within a
narrow band of impulses and motivations, revolving endlessly
around the same old blocks or obstructions within the personality.

A principal obstruction is sexuality. As Lee Lozowick points
out in the present book, the sexual revolution has failed to truly
liberate us and make us happier. Why? Because it has not demol-
ished the conventional, "flatland" understanding of life and
replaced it with the kind of deeper perspective of the human
situation that characterizes the teachings of the perennial philosophy. From those teachings we can glean the true place of sexuality in the scheme of things—not as a mere biological or
psychological function but as an important and even sacred
aspect of humanness where body, mind, and spirit converge.

The 70 "secrets" forming the sections of this book are major
and minor "points" about life—insights that remain closed to
conventional folk who seldom consider their own existence to
the point where they are struck by the sheer mystery of it all.
With his thought-provoking talks, gathered into a fine bouquet
in this volume, Lee Lozowick intends to do much more than
inform his readers. He wants to create in them a state of wonder
so that they can open themselves to higher wisdom and the possibility of genuine transformation in their lives.

Because we tend to be in a false relationship to our innermost Identity, which is Reality or the Divine itself, we also
habitually make a mess of our other relationships—not least

our relationship to the opposite sex. In fact, sex is today the area of the most pervasive confusion, deception, frustration, violence, oppression, and inner fragmentation.

In our perpetual pursuit of instant sexual gratification, we miss the whole wonderful mystery of eros. Lee Lozowick is not known for mincing words, and this book, like his other works, contains poignant straight talk. The reason for his candor is simple enough: Life is precious, and we must get on with what really matters. And what really matters is to win through to the insight that, contrary to popular belief, most of us live unhappy, unfulfilled lives, tending to look for happiness in the wrong places. When this insight has dawned on us, we can begin to walk the razor-edged spiritual path, which alone leads beyond suffering and all the pseudo-joys of everyday life to the blissful realization of our true Identity.

Lee Lozowick preaches neither asceticism nor hedonism but favors a middle path. He argues that since we have sexual organs, we should use them—but use them properly. For him this means that we engage sex, and in fact all other functions of our human personality, in deep communion with reality.

He criticizes what I have called "New-Tantrism"—the popular exploitation of Indian Tantra—because it mechanizes sex and depersonalizes individuals. He argues that communion is instinctual, that we innately "know the way through the labyrinth" and to what he calls our "organic innocence." Training—Tantric or otherwise—is unnecessary and would merely turn us into mechanics and our genitals into tools. What we need to do, though, is remove our obstructions, and here the present book offers important practical advice.

Before we try our hand at Tantra, Lee Lozowick recommends that we work on our intimate relationships, make them human. Thus we must discover the difference between chemical love (fatal attraction), emotional love (socially imprinted habits) and conscious love (which is geared toward voluntary self-transformation). So long as orgasm is the purpose of a relationship, we will never know the Man or the Woman in our partner but will remain at the surface of the personality.

I should emphasize here that 95 percent of Tantra has nothing whatsoever to do with sex. On the contrary, there is a strong penchant for celibacy in most Tantric schools. Left-hand Tantra, which involves sex, is the exception rather than the rule. And even in left-hand Tantra, conservation of the semen is practiced.

With characteristic humorous bluntness, Lee Lozowick puts it this way: "Tantra is a lot more than just sexual diddling in a ritual format." He too favors the conservation of orgasmic energy through regenerative sex. The surplus energy created by conservation must be translated into work. Gradually, the nervous system learns to carry a higher "electric" load, which ultimately transports consciousness beyond the confines of the bodymind. As Lee Lozowick explains: Real sex is S*E*X or "Sudden Ego Exit."

Authentic sexual communion obliterates all the differences that separate one individual from the other. When real love happens, or is "created" in the heart, the ego magically disappears. We ought not to be intimidated by this prospect, for the ego is hardly worth worrying over. And what is more: Being endures. Love endures. This is the core message of Lee Lozowick's book and madcap life.

Lee Lozowick has chosen a difficult path—not because he teaches in crazy wisdom fashion, but because he teaches the kind of thing that so few ears are willing to hear. This makes him look like a fool in the eyes of the world. Yet, teachings like his will always be available in this universe. If one day they were to vanish, humanity would most certainly be lost. We need to hear of love and true happiness, of the Divine and our true Identity, and of the graceful help that is always extended to us by the masters.

Let's listen well, then, to Mr. Lee's wise counsel.

EDITOR'S PREFACE

by Regina Sara Ryan

A prophet, as the Judeo-Christian scriptures affirm, is rarely recognized in his own country. It is not surprising then that the European community (particularly in France and Germany) has responded with vigor to the teaching of the American Baul spiritual Master, Lee Lozowick, while many of his own countrymen (and women) have dismissed, overlooked, or been insulted by his words. Lee Lozowick is not an easy teacher. His teaching, while profoundly simple, is excruciatingly demanding since his dedication is to nothing less than complete, and permanent, annihilation into the Heart of God.

In the eyes of many of his peers, his friends, students, and contemporaries, Lee Lozowick is considered to be an "enlightened" being, although he personally loathes that description because of the connotations it holds in the spiritual scene of the day. He might also be called a Tantric Master—as the astute reader of this book will soon learn. Yet, he would more happily be thought of and remembered as a rock and roll singer (he is the lyricist and lead vocalist in the group *liars, gods and beggars*), a holy fool, or a slave to the Will of God.

His straightforwardness and even wildness should come as no surprise to anyone who knows anything about the Bauls of Bengal, the sect and tradition with which Lee Lozowick's teaching work is most closely aligned. While they are little known in the West, the Bauls of Bengal have distinguished themselves, over a five-hundred-year history, by their passionate, iconoclastic approach to religion and spirituality, their ecstatic poetry, music and dance in praise of the Divine Beloved, *maner manush,* who indwells in each one's heart, and the closely-guarded esoteric sexual practices which are encoded in their songs. Because of their association with sexual sadhana, as well as the fact that most Bauls live as beggars, radically relying upon God for their existence and singing for their meager livelihood, even in India the Bauls are considered outcasts in polite society. Reputed by many to be sexual perverts, the Bauls' practices are enough to send religious traditionalists running for cover.

For the first ten years of his teaching work, Mr. Lee (the name given to Lee Lozowick by his own teacher, Yogi Ramsuratkumar) did not seriously discuss with his own students and devotees the subject of sexual practice, except on random occasions. Instead, he focused his energies in working with them on the basic stages of spiritual life, thereby establishing a framework within which sexual practice could be held in a healthy and balanced way—hopefully free of the sensationalism, embarrassment and ignorance that surround such a charged subject within our Western culture.

Since 1984, however, with the first public recognition and

acknowledgement of his association with the philosophy and practice of the Bauls, Mr. Lee has spoken at length about the conditions necessary for Westerners to engage sexuality and relationship as a Path to God.

As Bhaskar Bhattacharyya so clearly explains in his excellent book, *The Path of the Mystic Lover: Baul Songs of Passion and Ecstasy* (Rochester, Vermont: Destiny Books, 1993, page 148), the central concept of the Baul way is that of "the truth within the Body." It is within the body, therefore, that "the Man of the Heart" *(maner manush)* the Divine Beloved lives. And, whether one is male or female, "to find the Man of the Heart one must first become Woman."

Lee Lozowick's interpretation of this profound, esoteric principle of "becoming Woman" in relationship to the Divine (a tenet found in the gnostic teachings of nearly every great spiritual tradition) is, perhaps, one of the most valuable contributions of this book. As he does with other core aspects of the spiritual path, Lee Lozowick takes this principle "to the streets"—he lays it out in ways that the Western mind and heart can begin to grasp, even suggesting some simple, foundation-level steps to begin to augment this understanding of "becoming Woman" into one's life.

But, this book is not about techniques for improving your sex life. Rather, it is about the possibility of using sex and our intimate human relationships as an entryway into a transformed life. If sex, in and of itself, is one's goal, one has seriously missed the point. If fully awakened existence, characterized by kindness, generosity and compassion, is one's aim, something of value will be found here.

As the final editor, bearing the responsibility of presenting this mass of data in a way that would be readily accessible to the reader, I came upon the idea of dividing it up into a progressive series of essays which I called "secrets" because that was what I felt being revealed to me when I first read this remarkable text. Mr. Lee seemed to like my schemata (at least he didn't object—one is often unsure exactly what the spiritual Master actually "likes").

So, we called the pieces *secrets*—not because no one has heard of them before, but because they are still hidden from our complete comprehension. In many ways, they are secrets obscured by their own obviousness. If we are lucky and our readers are clever, these secrets will produce the same reaction that one has when finding his eye-glasses on his own head when he has been searching for them, with frustration, for an hour.

They are secrets also because unless they can be understood in the context of a life of surrender and sacrifice (unfortunately two dirty words in our time) they will never be grasped. There is an initiation required for the unlocking of these secrets—one that requires getting on one's knees (metaphorically at least, if not literally) and crawling through a very small opening, perhaps as tight as the birth canal. When Jesus said "...it is harder for a rich man to get to heaven than for a camel to pass through the eye of a needle..." he was not necessarily talking about the financially wealthy. He was more likely addressing those of us who are so learned, erudite even, so accomplished, and so experienced, that we are unwilling to lay down all of our assumptions in order to see, as if for the very first time, something we have lived with all our lives. Unless you, reader, are willing to do that, this book will annoy you at least, outrage you at best! The crazy-wise approach of this tantric Master will provoke your sensibilities, whatever they are. Without "beginner's mind" you will throw this book away as useless garbage. Don't say I didn't warn you!

Secrets, yes, but also these essays could have been called "clues"—hints, pieces of a puzzle, directions. These are not developed treatises. For the rational mind that will be a source of great frustration—it wants the scientific method, a linear progression, a step-by-step system. Although this manuscript has been significantly edited from the Master's original spoken words to provide some logical sequencing of his ideas, even so, this editor has found that it is quite impossible to get Mr. Lee to give the "whole story" about anything. Why? Because of his compassionate ruthlessness in the communication of the Truth.

Lee Lozowick will not compromise. He knows that others have already laid out this Path, with neon lights pointing to its essence, and still humans remain in the dark about their own nature and their denial system that keeps this "endarkenment" in place. He knows that by relying on the techniques presented in a book alone, people have proceeded to become good technicians while missing the whole point of the spiritual journey— which is to die to all one "thinks" one is and thus to become a being of knowledge. Lee Lozowick knows too that unless one comes to have this knowledge "in the body," as the Baul way indicates, and that unless one comes to these conclusions on one's own, they will be of no value. Awakening the body is a matter of experience, not intellectual, logical input.

This Master's style, therefore, is to drop crumbs (clues) and to wait, allowing time for them to be discovered, examined, eaten and finally digested; time for the truth to be recognized in the body!

If one approaches love and sexuality with all the answers, or even with Lee Lozowick's answers, one will attempt to fit one's experience of reality into some paradigm. If, on the other hand, one has only a treasure map with a few landmarks indicated, one is indeed fortunate. Such a map will give general assurance that one is moving in the right direction, but will leave one free to choose which particular highway will best suit one's needs in the journey, as well as how much time to spend along the way. While there is an urgency to this task, it is not an urgency created by time as we generally conceive of it. The value of Mr. Lee's approach is incomparably significant in this day and age when the "secrets of the ages" are packaged in week-end seminars and held up for a reasonable price to anyone with nothing better to do, or the money to buy. Tantric workshops are growing in popularity and availability throughout the industrialized world. Yet, few leaders of these workshops or authors of books on the subject are taking the gross insensitivity of the Western psyche into account in offering Tantric practices. These advanced methodologies are well and good for one who has been born and raised in a culture in which religious rite, archetypal correspondence, and the permeation of the sacred into every aspect of existence is the order of the day. We in the West have little or no precedent for the incorporation of these elevated approaches. We therefore think we can take on the form, distinguishing ourselves in sexual sophistication as if we were involved in some Olympic competition. In this domain, Americans (and Westerners in general) operate with a handicap so great as to almost disqualify them from participation all together. The illness of our Western psyche, and the sickness of our materialistic approach to everything from business to spirituality, must first be addressed if we are to gain any foundation here.

Coming from the streets, as do the Bauls, Mr. Lee knows, firsthand, the condition of this diseased psyche. His raw insight and ruthless criticism make this book, *The Alchemy of Love and Sex,* a provocative and refreshing addition to the literature on this subject. He refuses, moreover, to cater to our sensational or prurient interests and voyeurism in the sexual arena and will deliberately insult us to prevent that from happening. But, at the same time, he will use these very elements of the underworld as an entryway, prodding us (like cattle at times) to tell the hard truths about why we aren't happy, and why our lives aren't working despite our being immersed in the sexual, pleasure machine.

How to Use This Book: Because this is not pre-digested food, the material in this book needs to be chewed—even gnawed at, at times. My own experience is that reading it too quickly will leave me with a feeling of having overeaten, and reading it for "facts" will be a discouraging endeavor. Given time, approached with the necessary precautions for handling any potentially incendiary material, however, I guarantee that the reader will be richly rewarded for his or her efforts. It has been that reward for me.

Ideally, I recommend that this book be undertaken as a study guide for couples. Read the passages together, or aloud to one another. Pause for reflection and discussion. And be particularly alert whenever you hear yourselves saying: "Well, that's not *us* he's talking about!" That should be your biggest hint that something of value exists for you below the surface of your disinterest or your feeling of being offended.

Another valuable use of this material would be within the context of a couple's group. Meeting once a week, or once a month, the topics presented here should provide adequate motivation for study and discussion for a long time. This book is not an answer, remember. Rather, it is a book of secrets—given as clues which you must explore for yourselves, and then enhance by following together.

Whether one is living with a partner or not, engaged in sexual intimacy or not, however, this book will be extremely worthwhile. A single person will profit from these descriptions as much as any couple, and, as one will feel as he or she reads on, Mr. Lee has taken singles into account throughout his treatments. The energy of intimacy that he speaks about is applicable to all—to one's friends, family members...everyone. The point is to "become Woman" in relationship to life. . . all of life.

This book will point in that direction.

THE *Alchemy*
OF LOVE AND SEX

PART I

Root and Foundations

Since birth, the psychological and spiritual confusion of our culture has undermined what should have been a natural ease in relationship to others. We are, therefore, grossly unaware of the forces that motivate our actions, alienated from the body's organic wisdom, and handicapped in our sexuality. The secrets contained in Part I lay the groundwork necessary for understanding the rest of the material in this book.

Introduction

Philosophically, there is nothing that exists that is not God. That's fine and it's true. But practically, when human beings need to earn a living, find comfort, relate to one another and appreciate elegance, art, and so on, philosophical truisms are meaningless. My particular form of Teaching has to do, first, with considering the obstacles that keep us from realizing the Divine, not with speaking a lot of sweet and inspiring poetry about God which doesn't make a difference in people's lives. I am very practical, grounded, and direct in terms of what we need.

The nature of the Divine is dualistic in the sense that all manifestation is made up of attracting opposites. Energetically, then, men and women are like positive and negative electrical poles, or like the north and south polarities of a magnet. Essentially, men and women should attract one another. But, the north pole of a magnet doesn't have a prick, and the south pole doesn't have tits, and so people have other things to consider, besides energetics, that complicate what could and should be a very simple and clear process.

Even God doesn't have a sense of humor dark or sarcastic enough to make men and women essentially antagonistic. So, men shouldn't be a problem to women and women shouldn't be a problem to men, but unfortunately this is all too common. If men don't solve the *koan* of women and if women don't solve the *koan* of men, then we can forget about understanding the nature of God. That is why I have written this book.

The sexual revolution has hit the Western world like a storm, and yet people are more unhappy in sexual relationships than ever before. Now, even though people can buy every kind of electrical contraption, and all sorts of books and movies about "how to do it," people are "doing it" worse than ever before. Recently I was looking through a popular German magazine all about tantric workshops and "finding bliss through tantra." And I thought that the whole issue was one of the worst excuses for self-masturbatory indulgence I had ever seen. In these workshops people get to look at other people naked, and then to pat themselves on the back and say, "Aren't I great? Aren't I good at sex?...and free?...and wonderful?" But, as far as I'm concerned it's all shit—exhibitionism, voyeurism, and pre-adolescent immaturity. Listen, the Divine is not discovered by becoming more and more "far out." The Divine is discovered by becoming optimally normal.

Men will always be a mystery to women, and women will always be a mystery to men. When one discovers that mystery through experience, and if the mystery is allowed to exist as mystery, one has really discovered something. Becoming great sexual technicians is the fastest way to destroy the mystery. For instance, if a man is with a woman and able to feel her mystery, and she starts telling about her anatomy so that she can have more orgasms, something about that makes the mystery unappetizing.

Yet, to a frustrated and dissatisfied man or woman, a partner who is a good technician may seem like a really successful partner, but that is a veneer that fades very quickly. Likewise, if one simply wants to be fairly proficient at life, and completely and unavoidably separate from God, then one should look to become a good technician; but no degree of technical proficiency will effect communion with God.

Of course, a good technician is quite capable of igniting a few nerve endings in the brain, and that might *look* like God, or even *feel* like God. But any kind of experience, no matter how ecstatic, that does not transform the experiencer into someone who essentially knows how to be with children...how to be with their family members...how to be with their mates in a loving, deeply caring way...how to be with all of life...is not God! Natural and ordinary life, the way it is, is the alchemical crucible—the space in which transformation happens.

The Divine is not meant to be discovered in heaven. If the Divine was meant to be discovered in heaven, we would *be* in heaven and not here. And, despite the philosophy that the kingdom of heaven is "here and now," and that we have to make our lives here heaven, I'm sorry to have to tell you that this ain't heaven!

Secret 1: The Imprint of God is Woman

Psychologists tell us that children perceive the world non-dualistically for the first several months of life, at least.

But practically, they are totally dependent on "Mama." If they are hungry, they cry, and Mama is there. If they are cold or hurt or lonely, some "other"—Mama—is there. But a child doesn't see Mama as being separate from himself or herself, as coming from "out there" to give food or comfort. To a child, Mama is like an extension of the child's own body. The child's world is Mama.

At a certain age, perhaps six or seven months, the child's perceptions begin to change. He or she begins to see Mama "over there"—the Great and Mysterious Other; God.

The child doesn't see or make intellectual or scientific distinctions between "woman" or "man." Rather, he or she gets a whole, organic imprint (mental, physical, psychic...) of essential "woman-ness" or essential "man-ness." And the imprint the child gets of woman is so strong that the child sees Mama as God. It is understandable. What does Mama offer? Touch, warmth, attention, care. It's not the same for Daddy. He didn't carry the child; Daddy didn't feel life inside him; and the child didn't bond organically to Daddy in the way he did to Mama.

No matter what we want to think or say about it, a doting Daddy is not the same as a loving Mama. Typically, men like to pick up their child once in a while (when they have nothing better to do). When my son was little, I liked to look at him almost as much as I liked to touch him. There's something mind-blowing about babies, especially about your baby. I would stand and look at him in the crib, but I wouldn't pick him up and hold and cuddle him. Even when men do touch their children, it is not like a woman's touch. It isn't possible to be the same.

So, when the child looks at Mama and feels "That's God," that doesn't happen on a level of self-reflective conscious awareness. That imprint is one of pure, primal, organic instinct.

If the child is female, she instinctually feels, "I've got the same imprint. When I grow up I'm going to have to be God... Damn, that is a heavy responsibility." And it is! The imprint says: "I'm God—serve, serve, serve, and serve some more." The imprint says to take care of the whole damn world. It's a hell of a job to be God! Who in their right mind would want that responsibility? Nobody. Yet, the little eight, nine, or ten-month-old girl already knows, "One day I'm going to have to be responsible for being God because I am, in my essence, WOMAN." Most men are still children (or at best adolescents) at the emotional level. Somehow the little girl knows that, and feels the profound woundedness of the society—a woundedness that only God can heal. Such an awesome responsibility! And woman grows up with that imprint very, very deep.

What happens to a male child? At the point when he's starting to realize duality he gets an imprint from "God"/Mama that says, "I'm a boy. I don't have the same imprint as Mama. I'm not sure I like that. I wanna be God. I wanna be. I wanna be."

The lack of education in relationship to this issue has caused untold misery and violence, not to mention the unconscionable moral, social, psychological, psychic and spiritual imbalances in our contemporary world. Based on this lack, men are *trained* to be God as the patriarchal reaction to the undeniable and organic fact that woman *is* God.

Paradoxically though, men grow up trained to be God while inside they say: "I'm not God. Woman is God." What kind of psychological reaction do you think that causes? Anger, frustration, guilt, self-doubt, fear, defensiveness, and more. And what do these internal conflicts cause? Corresponding pain, violence, abuse and blindness. Men put women "down" by demeaning, hurting, brutalizing, and taking advantage of them. These are men's ways of trying to ignore or forget what they know to be true, bodily.

Adolescent reactivity against the goddess takes the form of denying the Truth of Her.

Certainly there are some more sensitive men around than the ones I've just described. Yet even so, many are unaware of all the subtle psychological recoil that leaks (or creeps) out of the cracks. The whole male psychological dynamic is a reaction against the conflict of being trained to be God and yet knowing that he is not.

Rhetorically, of course, and speaking non-dualistically, we are all God: men, women, all of creation. And rhetoric is all well and good, but what about the organic reality that moves us?

What about those 25 or 50 years' worth of denial and other unconscious ego strategies that have literally formed the body, mind, health, and all of our reactions and beliefs? A man can't just say, "Yes, we're all God," and expect to be healed, although that would be nice and delightful. But it doesn't work that way. We've got to root out the unconscious motivations and transcend them in clarity and through the disintegration of life-negative habits. That is a lifetime operation.

The child lives and grows as a result of food that it receives from Mama, and that is obviously not going to change. Men can't nurture with physical milk, with nutritional sustenance from their own bodies, as women can. (Maybe it's different on some other planet, but on earth, as long as *homo sapiens* are around, children will get suckled by Mama.) The imprint of the sustainer, of where life comes from, is still going to be woman.

The Divine Mother has been seen in the great spiritual traditions as the nurturer of the world, and in a limited sense as the nurturer of mankind. In Sanskrit they even call the woman goddess, Ma. For Ramakrishna[1], Kali Ma (a form of the Divine Mother) was the favorite deity. Ramakrishna so loved Kali that he even became a woman in practice and consciousness for a time.

He wore woman's clothing, lived among the women, and acted like a woman. The women, in turn, really loved and accepted him as one of them. He treated every woman like the Divine Mother. Even if dirty beggar women would come to the temple, Ramakrishna would bow down at their feet because they were the Mother, Kali.

Every woman was Kali. It wasn't that he liked women as different from or polar opposites to men. It was that he loved the Goddess.

Wouldn't it be nice if men could grow up with the imprint of reverence for the Divine Mother—the reverence she deserves for being the sustainer of the world? If it were not for Shakti we would not be here. (If it were not for Shiva we would not be here either, but if there were only Shiva, and not Shakti—which is a purely hypothetical situation, a concept of there being only *void*—that would be a very dull existence.)[2]

Wouldn't it be interesting if men were so mature and natural in their maleness that a true masculine imprint were passed on too? It is hard to imagine such a society because it is not in our middle-class experience. We don't yet know what it would be like if men and women honored women as Woman, as Shakti, and honored men as who they are, essentially. I'd like to see a group of people living together with genuine recognition of that, without regard for the psychological mechanisms that prompt men to belittle women, and women to respond through either fear or anger. Yes, I would.

---

1 Ramakrishna was an 18th century Indian (Hindu) saint known for his devotion to the Goddess Kali.

2 Shiva/Shakti - In Hinduism, the archetypal male and female aspects of the Divine referring to Context or consciousness (Shiva), and form and manifestation (Shakti).

Secret 2: Loved or Not Loved

Everybody grows up from the beginning with one of two primal relationships to life: "I'm loved" or "I'm not loved." That is why bonding with both mother and father is so important. If children are strongly bonded only to the female or only to the male, they may grow up feeling loved, but be personally and psychologically one-sided. If they are not bonded in the proper way, right away during the first two months, they will grow up feeling primally unloved. All of life will be an attempt to get this missing love, even if there is a loving influence. Later on, it's a bitch to re-do the first two months! Close to impossible!

Werner Erhard has expressed this dilemma in terms of the "scarcity of love." If you are a child who feels unloved, when you get to be an adult even Real love in your life doesn't obviate the feeling that you can't get enough love. So, you become a love-addict. One side of that is promiscuity and another side of that is being weepy, super-emotional, cotton-candy-sweet or needing to be stroked all the time. (Those kinds of people always have lots of pets. They have little dogs with pink bows in their hair, and sweaters and booties. And don't you want to gag whenever you see them?)

So, we either have one of two dispositions: "I'm loved" or "I'm not loved." The "I'm loved" disposition basically allows us to have a certain kind of self-confidence, even though we may be neurotic in other areas. In the "I'm not loved" primal-life-disposition we are always craving for some kind of proof that we are loved.

Secret 3: Man is Angry; Woman Is Afraid

Receptivity is the major feminine disposition and fear is woman's vital dilemma. The major masculine cramp[3], his vital dilemma, is anger. It's really quite obvious, once you think about it. Woman and man: fear and anger.

A woman wants to serve a Real Man. It doesn't mean that she wants to walk around all day with a little broom, whistling while she works—shining the dishes and polishing the windows—just being blissfully happy. Some women enjoy that, and service doesn't exclude that kind of activity. But, essentially, genuine service means the expression of feminine energy free of defensiveness and separation. To avoid confusion and controversy, then, we could say that Shakti (the archetypal feminine force in creation), wants to serve Shiva, (the masculine force), not because "she" as a separate individual desires to be appreciated, or thinks "he," as a separate individual, is such a perfect gentleman, but because Love in its ultimate sense *is* Service. The two cannot be separated. So, Woman wants to serve Man, and therefore wants to know the essence of her Divine, polar archetype.

In the face of this, for women, a feeling of fear arises, continually. More than simply an occasional manifestation, the perceptive observer will see that this fear is actually a deep

---

3 cramp - the primal knot of self-reference, referring to a whole range of physical, mental and emotional manifestations that are analogous to muscular cramping.

and pervasive mood. Even when a woman realizes there is nothing to be afraid of in any conventional sense, she will find that the fear is still present. What does she do about that?

One strategy is to attempt to eliminate the circumstances that appear to be creating the fear (which is often just like putting a bandage on a festering sore). Then, when the present feeling of fear goes away it is easy to forget that fear is actually underlying everything.

Another common alternative is to just "tough through" the times when this fear is being felt, immersing oneself in whatever else is going on, to whatever degree one can. Being tough is not a useful way of handling one's fear, although it does require at least some strength. Most humans, however, are too weak to do what is necessary for genuine healing.

Others attempt to forget their fear by obliterating the feeling itself. Drugs, alcohol, sex, and power are a few of the tools in this program of obliteration. Of course, the fear never actually gets destroyed—it just gets covered up, or masked. If you read *People Magazine,* for instance, movie stars are often asked, "What do you do when you feel depressed?" One woman replies: "Oh, I spend $30,000 at Neiman-Marcus or Saks 5th Avenue." And, she adds, "It always works. After a while I just feel great. I never wear all the clothes, shoes, or hats I buy, but I feel good. It's worth $30,000." The strategy is to suppress reality.

If you're not a rich movie star, you may try to obliterate your fear at a French bakery with Napoleons and eclairs, or you may use drugs or alcohol. In fact, the language used to describe states of addiction and intoxication—those means of creating artificial veils against reality—precisely label the condition in which you forget the dilemma. People speak of being "smashed," "wasted," "blown away," or "blind."

The truth is, however, that you can get as drunk or "high" as you want, but you always come back and remember. Every time you attempt to obliterate the thing that causes the fear, or when you declare war on it, or try to beat it up, it just gears up for defense. The fear becomes more apparent to you when you do "come down," and soon it becomes so obvious that it's consuming you that you must work even harder to try to forget it again.

Another way for a woman to "forget" her fear is by getting lost in her job or in her social life, until the next time that fear arises. Then she might say, "Oh, here it is again. If I just speed up the distractions fast enough, I'll get through it without having to really face it." And this kind of denial can go on for a lifetime.

Hopefully, there will come a point in a woman's life in which no distractions will work any longer. If she is lucky she will start to see the fear frequently, almost constantly, and then she will have to get more serious about confronting it.

The only enduring way of dealing with the fear is to recognize *what is prior to it,* and then to practice or live from that position. Find the root of the arising of this pervasive fear, and rest, or be conscious, there. Live there; dwell in that place. There is no "how to" instruction that is possible here.

The only way to finally transcend the fear that underlies your life and prevents your femininity from expressing itself (and nothing else will deal with the fear except on a temporary basis) is to realize *what is prior to it*, and to live in that realization as your state of being.

Even a momentary experience of resting in that place is better than nothing, but this is no final resolution. The fear can always recapture the field of battle, meaning it can consume your attention once again. Ultimately, I'm talking about residing in that place permanently, as a context of your life, not in a particular form that you might imagine or project.

• • •

Now on to the other half, or so, of humanity.

The mature way to deal with anger is to recognize that anger arises not as a function of circumstance (like being threatened), or from any outer, rational cause. Rather, anger for men is a function of the same primal disposition that fear is for women.

The obvious response to that, it seems to me, once a man has intellectually analyzed it (and that certainly doesn't do anything about the anger) is to enquire[4] about the arising of the anger:

"What am 'I' angry about?" he should ask himself.

—"Nothing, actually. It's just anger."

"But, there must be a reason somewhere," he might argue.

—"Yes, but the reason is old and completely irrelevant to anything that's going on now."

The same is true of fear. "There must be a reason for it," the woman demands.

Yes, there was a reason for the fear at one point, just as there was a reason for this underlying, pervasive anger at one point. (Not an objective reason, but a reason that made sense to ego in its formative period.) And those reasons are totally irrelevant to the content of our lives as adults. Yet we still respond like children who have been too harshly pulled off the breast or toilet-trained too soon, or like children who have had certain crimes inflicted on them. Even when we're mature adults we are still trying to make up for what happened when we were children.

In any case, the way to deal with either fear or anger is to realize that these dispositions are the primal considerations that you function with, defend yourself against, and express yourself with. Then, remember that you are always trying to

---

4   to enquire, or Enquiry - Traditionally, a form of spiritual practice in which the question "Who am I?" is used. In the teaching of Lee Lozowick that question becomes: "Who am I kidding?" It is used randomly in response to any feeling, thought or experience that arises. It is used to gain insight into one's true nature.

forget them. Finally, enquire about that disposition, without deluding yourself by identifying any of the superficial circumstances or manifestations in your life as cause for this feeling. (When things come up in your life that make you afraid or angry, those things are usually just the decoys.)

Keep in mind that I am not talking about the fear or anger caused by a natural or instinctual event. If someone you love is very ill, you fear for them. Suppose you walk out of a business appointment and notice that somebody has smashed your car. You get angry. I'm not talking about those kinds of fear or anger. I'm talking about the primal motivation, the essential dilemma, the vital feeling that remains present when there is no apparent reason for it, when the seeming reason for it disappears, or even after you see through the reason.

Don't compromise your own ability to be freely happy by making the false assumption that the things or circumstances in your life are the reasons for these feelings (either happiness or its opposites). For example, a woman might say, "Every time I really become vulnerable to a man, he leaves me, and that's why I'm afraid of relationship." Bullshit! Or, a man might say, "I gave her everything. I shared my life with her, and now look what she's doing to me in court. I'm angry." Those superficial explanations have nothing to do with the essential cramps of anger or fear.

● ● ●

How does one begin to rest in the disposition that is prior to the fear and the anger? We have to start somewhere and go a step at a time, otherwise it won't work. Start with training attention which will show you how often you are not resting in the disposition prior to anger or fear. Start training attention about how you use your mouth—with what you say to whom, how you say it, the tone in your voice, how often you say it. Begin to observe these things objectively, dispassionately, without drawing conclusions. If you notice that what comes out of your mouth is garbage, like constant complaining, you have to do something else. So, the first thing to do is to stop that kind of bad habit.

To fully rest in the context of freedom, however, there is no "how to" that applies. A free disposition is not something you attain, reach through effort, or master through work or apprenticeship. Rather, it's a matter of relaxing into, not growing into something. It's a question of distillation and refinement. What is left after distilling and distilling and distilling is Context[5], the essence of all this. The way to begin to distill qualities of life and refine one's presence is to begin to treat the anger and the fear as if they were not valid and justifiable. Every time we complain, "bitch," and withdraw from life, we reinforce those primal conditions.

Women tend to withdraw from life when the fear arises. They tend to sit in the corner and dwell in their own fear. They tend to shut-up, shut-off. When anger is present, men tend to validate it and support it by a kind of reverse camaraderie—lashing out and being destructive, abusing whomever is in front of them.

You begin to refine your life by starting to round off the rough edges. Do not do that by superimposing a sort of positive attitude on things, like: "Every day, in every way, I'm getting better and better." That will only encourage you to forget about the anger or fear for a time, or even for years.

The process is a matter of distillation and refinement. The anger and fear are already there. It is not the circumstances at all, by any stretch of the imagination, which cause them. So don't bother stretching the imagination.

5　Context - the texture or mood underlying form or content. When not capitalized, context refers to the feeling or underlying quality of an individual circumstance. When capitalized, Context refers to the condition of Surrender to the Will of God, as in the case of the spiritual Master.

Secret 4: Why Men Can't Cry
(and what women do about that)

Most men are angry. They are angry because they can't cry. It's much easier to be angry—there is an egoic pleasure in it. Anger is self-righteous, satisfying, and always has an object, real or imagined. This is not necessarily the case with sorrow.

Most men are simply not willing to walk around pervasively sad. Men like to know the "Why?" of things, they don't like to "just feel." So, the anger in men is the result of their inability—sometimes unwillingness, but mostly the inability—to cry, to grieve, to feel their sorrow, not just when the car gets wrecked, but beyond that, to genuinely cry because of racial remorse, to cry for their species, to feel the sorrow of God. (The way I'm discussing crying here is not simply the ability to shed tears. It's the ability to grieve, to feel deeply and with the whole body.)

Most women, however, react to men's anger as if it were unjustified, as if it were the anger of a little boy not getting his way, rather than looking at why men are angry. Women often presume that man's anger is controllable or superficial. Then men get more angry, or even violent. Now his anger has an immediate object—the woman who reacts to him! For example, a man comes home angry because he didn't get the raise he wanted at his job, and his wife gets disturbed by his anger. What does he do? He lashes out at *her*. It's a vicious circle.

Men rarely touch the depths of their own being that are connected to their sorrow. Instead, they use their relationships with woman as the focal point of their anger. Women become the projected cause of man's anger when they should be the solution. Woman, i.e. the Feminine[6], is the answer to his anger. Woman is the heart of sorrow in which true and complete healing is possible. Men get angry at feminists, and at many other things, as a distraction from the real source of their pain. Even when they believe that anger is somehow sinful and bad, many men will show sublimated or disguised anger in their demeaning treatment of women—by corporate power-tripping, or by becoming some kind of cop, official or otherwise. Such a man might bark orders at his secretary, like, "Get my coffee," even if the coffee is only two steps away from his own desk. It's a sign of his control and power (i.e. repressed anger) to have her get the coffee, however.

The usual psychological response to anger is, "If I'm angry I'm bad, therefore I shouldn't be angry," and that attitude gets translated into denial, or suppression, or possibly and even worse, into something "good." "If I can't not be angry," says the man, "I'll just justify my anger, in my own mind, and make it necessary and good."

Women play a crucial role in determining where a man's expressed anger gets directed. Since all men are born of and exist because of Woman, this deep unconscious reliance on the Feminine, both personally and in a cosmic sense, creates the basic stuff of masculine neurosis—the primal ego justification for misogyny and unconscionable patriarchal behavior. The simple, emotional expression of anger is perverted, therefore, into something else.

Typically, because anger is addressed towards women, women become offended or insulted, knowing intuitively that they are

---

6 The Feminine - One of the universal polarities, having to do with the manifestation and form of the Divine; may also refer to the essential and psychological characteristics in the human domain.

not the cause. Men are angry because they have ruled women for thousands of years and they know that they are not living in a way that is just, or true to the Divine Nature of Reality. At the psychological level, men feel powerless in the face of having power, yet are unclear and unconscious about this. They are unable to do anything about their powerlessness except be angry, suffer the effects of this anger, and be manipulated by feelings of impotence and frustration.

Today, women are trying to get back, trying to recapture their rightful place in the energetic matrix of human life on earth. But women are as unclear and unconscious as men, and so their instinctual drive towards rebalance is often generated through a field of anti-male, emasculating, and dominating rhetoric and action. (Women say they want equality, but they actually want to re-establish the culture of the Goddess that is the source of true Wisdom and sacred life.)

Men's feelings of powerlessness are all true on a superficial level, but deeper than that, anger in men is the result of a failure to grieve for the loss of the Truth. If a woman were able to understand that her man's anger was not really the result of not getting the raise but rather because of a certain emotional blockage, or cramp, if she could refrain from taking his anger personally or being offended by it, that would make a big difference in the dynamic between them. (It wouldn't necessarily transform the anger, but in many instances it would help the man come to balance and resolve about the issue.) If she could provide nurturance to the part of him that is crying out beneath his words, instead of reacting to the part that is shielding his true woundedness, that would be transformative. (But I know that kind of sensitivity is very difficult. Anger doesn't encourage empathy and compassion as sorrow does. Anger does degenerate into violence so easily.)

If women could relate to men's anger and "take a stand"[7] for the man's ability to grieve, in some cases (if not in every case), men would feel this acknowledgement. They would grieve and allow themselves to be nurtured and that would completely eliminate the misguided representation of man's heartful sorrow.

When a man is involved in his own process, and especially if he is feeling disturbed and going inward, the first thing that women usually want to do is "mother" him. She will try to be affectionate, misunderstanding that what the man most wants is to be left alone to honestly grieve. Often, if the man is given even three minutes—just a little bit of space—he would be available and present to her again.

Psychologically, men need space and women need assurance. When a woman is grieving she wants the man to reassure her, to provide comfort and support through touch and contact. She wants him to say, "I still love you, I still want you, you're beautiful," even if she looks like "death warmed over."

A man doesn't want that same type of assurance. A man wants space. He just wants to work it out for himself. Men can work things out fast if they are left alone. If men were allowed to grieve, in their own way, a lot of their negative moods in relation to women would be eliminated.

Sorrow is not the root of anger, but anger masks sorrow. If anger were not used as a distraction, sorrow would naturally arise, and this sorrow would be greatly humbling and awesomely transforming. This genuine sorrow is grief for the human condition: the sorrow of realizing the frustration of the Divine...recognizing the impossibility of perfection in relation to God...seeing ourselves as who we really are, stripped of our ego pretenses and free of our projections, wishes, hopes, and

---

7 take a stand - a phrase popularized by Werner Erhard. To take a stand is to make a strong commitment to support something or someone, or to be willing to be responsible for something.

fears. To live on the basis of *this* Reality would be so freeing and life-confirming that nothing else would be desired.

Because that Real sorrow is so consuming, however, anger tries to avoid it. Anger is the psyche's (or ego's) response to the intimation of its own meaninglessness, or of its lack of autonomy, in contrast with the "Everything" or "Allness" of the Divine.

Sometimes, we relate to that sorrow as if it were ordinary sadness, having to do with a specific issue in our lives. Once you have felt the "genuine heart of sadness"[8] as Chögyam Trungpa referred to it, you know experientially that it is different from ordinary sadness. But before you know, as a whole-bodily experience, the difference between ordinary sadness and the "genuine heart of sadness," you can't define it. Intellectual understanding alone is simply too narrow and limited.

So, we must not mistake usual sorrow—honest sadness at a real loss or some pain of personal human suffering—for this sorrow of the Bodhisattva[9]. To fail to make this distinction is to forget God once again.

---

8 genuine heart of sadness - described by Tibetan Buddhist teacher, Chögyam Trungpa, in: *Shambhala, The Sacred Path of the Warrior* (Boston, MA: Shambhala Publishing, 1984). Through the path of meditation the "warrior" experiences a raw vulnerability. The heart becomes exposed and is therefore deeply touched by the condition of others.

9 Bodhisattva - In Buddhism, a being or deity who is the embodiment of compassion. A Bodhisattva vows to save all sentient beings from the illusion of existence before he himself is saved.

Secret 5: Familiarity Can Breed Contempt

In the Middle Ages in Europe there was a particular movement of chivalry in which men took a vow never to actually have a physical relationship with a woman, but only to view a particular woman as their ideal object of adoration—so pure as to be worshipped, but untouchable. They would write love notes and poetry and beg her permission to be worshipped, to accept their devotions.

Men and women in our times tend to have an interesting dynamic of some slight similarity. When apart from one another, their sensitivity to the essential energy dynamic that exists between male and female, is very acute. Separated, they can readily experience feelings of tremendous integrity, responsibility, and clarity towards each other. They can develop the clear intention of being together with service, compassion, generosity and gentleness.

As long as they are not confronted by the superficial, five-sense stimuli, it is always much easier for them to "see" or instinctually sense the pure and perfect archetypal essentials of the other—male or female.

So, paradoxically, men and women intend to relate to one another based on the essential relationship of energy that each of them represent; but when they get together, ego tends to use the physical dynamic to create a circumstance that is completely selfish or self-centered, manipulative instead of relational.

Let me give you an example. Let's say a man and a woman

spend a day apart, and during that day they occasionally think about one another. The man thinks, "When I come home, it'll be nice to see my lady. I can give her a big kiss hello. I've missed her all day, and we'll talk a little bit and sit down. I'll put some candles on the table and bring her a flower and it'll be real nice." Perhaps the woman thinks, "I'm going to come home a little early and cook a special dinner. I know the way to a man's heart is through his stomach."

So, they meet at the end of the day, full of intention towards elegance, sensitivity, and communion. The man walks in and, having a terrible, weird sense of humor, says to the woman who has been cooking an extraordinary meal for hours,

"What stinks, honey?" Then he looks at the roast in the oven and says, "Don't tell me that's the dog. My God, I was just getting to like that furry, little shit!" Well, the woman is somewhat used to his sense of humor, so it is annoying, but she says, "Ha, ha, ha, isn't that funny? Just go get cleaned up and get ready for dinner." He says, "Okay," and doesn't think a thing about it as he waltzes off to the bathroom, happy as a pig in shit, to wash his hands, or more likely to admire himself in the mirror.

A few minutes later the man comes out of the bathroom and goes to sit down at the table. Now the woman says, "No, no. I want you to sit *here*," indicating a different chair from the one he is choosing. He says, "Can't I sit *here*?" She says, "No, no, it's very important, you have to sit *here*." Then he gives in and goes over and sits down where the woman has directed him, but meanwhile he's getting a little annoyed too. "After all," he is thinking, "a man's home is supposed to be his castle, isn't it? And the king ought to be able to sit where the hell he wants, shouldn't he?

At last she brings out the dinner, and soon she too is waltzing and maybe even singing, around him, in the way that happy and affectionate women do. She's taking care of him, mothering and doting. Well, there's nothing that makes a man angrier than when a women tries to take care of him as if he were two years old. So, as you can imagine, by the time dinner is over, both of them have got big agendas of issues. They are both annoyed, even though they are being polite to one another because the "goodies" come later. But, the tension is definitely building up.

While they were apart from one another there were no annoyances at all, just simple love and appreciation, and they had the intention of being different in relationship to one another. But once together, the habitual and uninspected psychological trigger-mechanisms completely obscured the best of intentions.

Men have this saying about women, "Women, you can't live with them, and you can't live without them." Women have this saying about men, "Men, what can you do with them? They're all such little boys, but they're such cute little boys. They're just so adorable!" It doesn't matter if a man is built like me, (looking like an abstract Picasso) he still wants to walk in and have the woman think, "My hero!"

A man may at times know what a woman wants, or how women want to be treated, or what the "Essential Woman" needs, and vice versa. Yet the dilemma is in how to resolve the struggle between what we feel in sensitive and clear moments with the incredible power of ego to immediately blind us with its own devious intentions. (You shouldn't make any mistake about ego's neurotic intentions. Maybe "devious" is even too light a word. Ego's entire intention is to maintain its survival, and it will destroy anything that gets in its way! Anything—including the body itself. Many examples of suicide demonstrate this in psychologically predictable ways.)

Three things are particularly useful in working with this dichotomy, this dilemma: Understanding, Intention or Resolution, and the Discipline to pay the price. The first thing that we need to work on is a clear, precise understanding of the mechanics of habit—of how sex becomes a powerful tool for manipulation of self or others rather than a pleasurable element of relationship. This must include the recognition that change doesn't happen overnight, and that change and progress happen in the circumstance one is presently involved in, not somewhere else.

The second element of working with the dilemma of men and women has to do with cultivating the attitude that resolution comes through practice, experience, self-observation and the intention to be different. It does not come through some kind of extreme, "do or die," ascetic practice.

The third necessary element is the willingness to give attention and discipline to the wish to become a whole human being, true to the energy of one's gender. And we need to make the resolution of this dilemma worth the price that needs to be paid. If every time you feel a bit lusty you "get laid," you will never deal with the issue of Right Relationship; you will never engage Real Masculinity and Real Femininity; you will never integrate the health and vitality of your own anima/animus.

So, getting to the point of being able to be with a lover or companion without tension is a matter of practice, study, experience, and most primarily, the proper context. There's no fast way to transform not only a lifetime of habits, but many, many centuries of history and tradition.

Secret 6: The Secret of the Preying Mantis

The preying mantis is an interesting breed of insect to study for a certain cannibalistic behavior. The female preying mantis eats the male after she is impregnated. She starts with the head, and finally eats the best part—the nice, meaty body. Sometimes the male preying mantis continues to copulate even for hours after its death, while the female is eating it's body.

A lot of men feel, at some deep place in their psyches, that this is exactly what happens when they are with a woman. They think that their life gets eaten, and that they are being emasculated by women. This feeling is not directed at any one woman, necessarily. Rather, it's a psychological, even pathological, energy dynamic of male with female.

Men have a violent aggressiveness towards women which gets directed towards the "denying female" of the species in general—that is, against the "devourer," the "smotherer," which is an element of all women. This male aggressiveness is directed at a neurotic manifestation of women, not at the archetypal shadow character (which is a necessary part of the female energy).

In reality, the Feminine does consume the Masculine, and any man in his right mind would beg to be truly surrendered to That—to Her. Women don't want to emasculate men. But men are just so childish. What's a woman to do when she realizes that the thirty-year-old guy that she had set all her hopes on is just a bundle of reactions and "buttons waiting to be pushed?" It's so depressing. Men resent it when women act like mothers towards them, but they also don't fathom that they elicit that dynamic through their own immature activity.

Male aggression towards women is not true of all men to the same degree, but it is common enough because most men were not properly mothered in a natural way. Men, therefore, tend to grow up defining their lives in reaction to weak mothering rather than out of the strength of knowing who they are, as men. They grow up at the effect of forces that they feel they should be master of. Instead of blaming their own mothers for that, men blame the entire culture of women instead. But this effect happens so early in a male's life, and is so strategically forgotten, that by the time he is an adult the man has developed a social consciousness which overshadows his primal, subconscious patterns. He doesn't know that he is actually enjoying female company for the conquest, the "hunt." He has learned so well how to be socially acceptable that he represses this conflict between his essential beingness and his conditioning. (And, there is also a level at which men truly enjoy feminine energy, company, and nature. But, I'm making a point here.)

Nancy Friday wrote a book called *My Secret Garden* (New York: Pocket Books,1973) about women's sexual fantasies. It was a wild, terrifying book, and also wildly successful. Then she did a book on men's sexual fantasies, gathering material by advertising in magazines and through questionnaires.

Overall, I thought the book on male fantasies was unimaginative, definitely dry and uninteresting when compared to the women's book. And you might be shocked at how many men have fantasies that involve doing violence to women after making love to them. (Of course most men never seriously engage those fantasies in practice because they have some rudimentary conscience.) Men also can't openly communicate their fantasies because these are usually too much in conflict with their moral natures and their heartful instincts. Typically, men are repressed and separated from genuine, spontaneous masculinity.

Women's sexual fantasies, on the other hand, consistently took the form of bondage, of having men subdue them, or of being slaves to the man's every whim. It's interesting that women tend to have fantasies, not of castrating men (as men fear), but rather of serving them, in submission. Considering how brutalized women have been in the last several thousand years or so by men, it is very interesting.

In order for a boy to develop a strong sense of his own masculinity a type of bonding must take place when he is an infant. What commonly happened in our day, however, was that mommy went to the hospital, the baby was born and immediately taken away and put in an incubator. Daddy got to come in and hold the baby, but only for a minute or two. Breastfeeding was discouraged, as was "natural childbirth," and the prevalent attitude was one of not wanting to be bothered. "Just get the baby on a bottle so he or she can be trained to a certain time schedule, then mommy won't be inconvenienced." Needless to say there was almost never any bonding to the male parent—for boys or girls.

Babies should be bonded to both parents, right from the beginning, and then have male company on a regular basis so they can develop strong and consistent role models. Affection should be freely shown in any environment with children— affection between men, between women, between partners in a couple, and of course between the parents and the children. One of the most damaging things that can happen to a young boy is for affection to be shown by his father to his mother but not by his father to him. Or, for his mother to show affection to his father but not to him. Some people find it easier to give affection to their mate than to a child, which is unfortunate but understandable when you consider how many adults never received adequate nurturing or bonding as children.

• • •

A positive approach or resolution to deal with the violence men feel towards women is, first, not to animate it—that is, for instance, not to give the lady a black eye...or anything like that. This holding back will, if the man is disposed towards his own healing, act as a magnifying glass to his deeper underlying dynamics. It will goad him towards the unemotional clarity that allows space for change, and also will provide him with access to the actual tools for such change.

Intellectually, it's easy to understand the psychological reasons for violence and aggressiveness, but to act on the basis of great insights a man must deepen both his self-observation and his discipline. The only way the dynamic of aggressiveness gets diffused is if the man is able to be in a situation in which aggressiveness arises and yet still rest, in consciousness, in a place that is prior to the aggressiveness or violence.

Enquiry is the way to continually deepen, in stages, the level of consciousness at which one is perceiving things. One wants to get to the level prior to where this dynamic of aggressiveness was established. So, every time the dynamic comes up, one enquires: "Who am I kidding?" in relationship to it. For example: "I don't really hate women... Who am I kidding?" The practice becomes more natural and effective as one uses it, and will even arise spontaneously, but one must use it in an intentional way at first.

Aggressiveness and violence are not a "given" for the species. While you may have inherited some of it, aggressiveness and violence are still just behavioral conditioning.

Like many political problems, there are no immediate solutions to this dynamic of aggressiveness and fear between men and women. But, if we consider the problem and commit ourselves to the resolution of it deeply enough, maybe in several generations there will be a sufficient number of people who have defined it clearly, recognized it in themselves, and are educated properly enough to pass on this education. For the time being, the most we can hope for is to recognize our own motivations and defuse the aggression in them. Perhaps then we can shift the context of our responses to one of Surrender to the Will of God[10].

---

10 Will of God - The natural expression of universal divine movement. God's Will is therefore not an edict inscribed on stone to which we must bend our own will, but an intuitive sense of "rightness" to which we may chose to respond in every unique circumstance. To be "surrendered" is to have no choice but to recognize our response as appropriate in every moment to the exact needs of that moment.

Secret 7: Proving Ourselves to Mama

To be a Man "with a capitol M" as G.I. Gurdjieff[11] would have said, literally has to do with whether one has still got to prove himself to his parents. (This is not the only ingredient, but it is one of them, for sure.)

If you are of the male species and you still have to prove yourself to your mama, you are going to try to prove it to every woman with whom you get intimate, and to most of those with whom you don't. (You may do this by a physical posture alone, which means as much to the subconscious as a sexual experience.) That is hardly the way to be in right relationship, not only to a mate, but to half the human race. Even to your mama, that's not the way to be in relationship—to have to prove to her that you're okay, successful, independent, and "grown up."

Your mamas are always going to treat you like babies, even when you're forty-five years old, and even when they, or you, are dead. Proving yourself to your mama is not a matter of convincing her that you are an adult, because to your mama you're always going to be her little baby. This is obvious. It's not any esoteric secret.

To really prove yourself to your mama is to love her because she *is* your mama, just how she is, not how you want her to be, or wished she was when you were little. To convince her you're

---

11 Gurdjieff - a 20th-century Russian mystic, author, and teacher.

an adult at last and that you can make your own decisions is not only fruitless but highly impossible anyway. You prove yourself to your mama by loving her, truly loving her. Even when you achieve great fame, and when hordes of people come to bow at your feet and get your autograph, mama still thinks that you are her little baby. You never prove yourself to your mama by what you become, nor by who you are, but by whom she is to you.

Obviously, if you try to prove yourself to a mate, you can see the handicap that will be in the relationship. (What relationship?) Some men try to prove themselves to their mamas by being harsh and unrelational to their mates: "I'll show you that I'm independent and I'm not hanging on your coattails, lady." They never have a kind word. They never give in. Macho men never surrender to their mates (but still often get depressed when they orgasm, though they mightily deny it, most of all to themselves).

Some men try to prove themselves to mama by being supplicating and "sucking up" to women: "Yes dear, yes dear. Aren't I a good little boy? I do everything you say. And I never do anything wrong." And, "Yes dear, yes dear, I'm not making any mistakes this time...Mom...." Try this on a mate who wants you to be a man and see what happens. There are different ways of doing this, but obviously if you are trying to relate to someone directly as an equal, that's a pretty poor way of going about it. Have you noticed how many men marry women who are literal duplicates of their mothers? It's very common. A lot of men "marry" their mothers because they can't screw their mothers, or keep nursing at their age. But they can screw their wives and continue to be the dependent or rebellious children they always were. And they think that's love! "The relationship is going to work because I don't have to change," they feel subconsciously, "and my mother always loved me in spite of my weaknesses and so will my wife (new mother)." This is not typically the kind of stuff a couple would talk about with one another. This is about primal motivations that are usually so far from consciousness they are considered ridiculous if they ever rear their heads.

Women try to prove themselves to their mothers in similar ways: they use their mates. "If I run my man's life, then you'll know I'm capable. Then you won't treat me like a baby when I'm thirtysix years old, Mom."

If a woman were consciously trying to prove herself to her mother, that would be fine. If she were doing it with full awareness and attention, she could stop at anytime. But, if she pays close attention to the content of her relationships, she will see that they are mechanical and compulsive...totally compulsive. (And that's the very reason to engage spiritual life—because we don't act intentionally. If we really knew what we were doing, we wouldn't need spiritual life.)

Realizing that you "married your mother," you don't have to be shocked and think, "Oh my God, I've got to find somebody else. What an awful thing. I was thrust into this by some neurotic pattern." So what? Lots of us moved into relationships out of purely neurotic patterns. We can still make excellent relationships out of these if we deal with the relationship as it stands and obviate the neurotic pattern through clarity and wisdom.

Make peace with it. After all, how many people get a real chance to see the truth, and actually to resolve their unacknowledged, but constantly motivating, conflicts with adult reality. Without such resolution, marriage will be, at best, benign and gentle, but still founded on a lie; and at worst, it will be a nightmare of violence and denial doomed to "codependent hell" or practical failure...only to be repeated endlessly.

Change is not at issue. Experiences are not at issue. Deal with where you are and what you have, not with what would be or could be.

Secret 8: Reclaiming The Feminine

One of the most popular emphases in psychotherapy today is around "reclaiming the feminine." I think, however, that it is out of the domain of psychotherapy to attempt to deal with reclaiming the feminine. Instead, psychotherapy needs to deal with the sources (in childhood) of abuse, neglect, and shaming by ignorant adults.

The masculine is only diseased because of the state of the feminine. If the feminine were truly "reclaimed," nothing would have to be done with the masculine; it would be whole and healthy automatically. The whole problem is with having rejected the Feminine and its beauty, its fecundity, its depth, in favor of the masculine and its aberrated domination, manipulation, and power. The disease of the masculine is actually a reaction, a desperate attempt to assuage the profound guilt and shame of having so abused and demeaned the Feminine. This disease is an attempt by man to forget the impotence he experiences without the Feminine as the context of, and partner in, his reality.

To actually reclaim the Feminine in a whole-bodily way requires a connection to a source in which the Feminine is already sacred and in its proper role.

Many people have experiences of communion with that Feminine, but in terms of entering into it as one's context, entering into the stream of its blessings in a permanent way, I think one needs to be introduced into the stream by one who is already there. The attempt to go into that stream under one's own power has got to be an attempt fraught with obstacles since any initiative can only come from that which isolates you from the source and has kept you from this source all your life, namely ego. So it's obviously a self-defeating process. Even though it is academically possible, it is practically impossible.

I view contacting the Feminine as contacting pure essence, the same as finding God. Someone who could do that, I would call a sorcerer, a devotee, an enlightened being, a warrior, or a shaman. Appropriate forms of psychotherapy can help clear us out, so that we can consider these possibilities which often don't dawn on us because the mind is so rigid. Therefore, psychotherapy can help us become right-brained—freer in our vast possibilities.

In the gross cultural context there have been a couple of thousand years of male domination and a couple of thousand years of the feminine being manipulated by that. We can't separate ourselves from our genetic memories. Everywhere we go, in whatever we do, we carry these memories around, and therefore the sparks will fly.

The first thing, then, in our ability to reclaim the feminine is to know how many hidden agendas we have (like the genetic memory that males dominate females), so that we develop a desire for healing, for wholeness. That in itself is a great step— one most people never make. Most people think, "Oh, I've just got this one little problem. It's no big deal." But it is!

Next, it's a matter of keeping these agendas in mind and creating a desire not to animate them, not to be so hurtful and foul. When you get to the root of the agenda, you won't have it anymore, ever. In the meantime, just don't move into circumstances unconsciously. Maintain attention, know you've got agendas, and know that you don't want them. That is bringing intention to the consideration. Then, Divine Influence[12] will

---

12 Divine Influence - The transformative power which aligns one who is vulnerable to it to the Will of God. It is tangibly made available through the spiritual Master.

take care of the situation…but not without your help. Divine Influence will provide the necessary ingredients to make those hidden agendas workable, instead of having them remain so unconscious that they kick into high gear before you have a chance to do anything about them.

What I'm suggesting isn't all that attractive to the masculine ego, especially. In fact, it's the least attractive thing. So, in the beginning you may have to make that consideration an act of will. It's like studying something you don't want to study because you've got to take a test. You just do it!

Perhaps we can't find Real Masculinity without Real Femininity. Before we've found real Femininity, all we'll do is react to the feminine. But if we were to submit to the Feminine, we might find the real masculine just sitting there in all its glory. That which we've been looking for all along is somewhere else than where we've been expecting to find it.

There are several approaches to submitting to the Feminine. One way is like Ramakrishna dressing up in women's clothes and living with women for a while, not just living with women but living *as* a woman. Another approach is from an internal disposition rather than from the form. To do that, you would consider the distinctions between the Masculine and the Feminine and encourage the qualities of the Feminine in your behavior and your moods. You establish a certain disposition towards the Feminine, rather than towards any human woman. You never know what might arise from that and you stay open to whatever it is that will show up.

But, don't dramatize this mood or this disposition, just be invisible with it. Don't tell everybody what you're doing.

Whether you are a man or a woman, surrendering to the Feminine is the process.

Secret 9: Develop A Passionate Love Affair With Life

You've got to take life by the *cojones* and let it sweep you up in its extravagance. There's generally too much "me"—too much ego—trying to take life and chew it up. Relax and let life smother you. Life will consume you if you let it. You're the ring on the carousel and life is coming around to grab you. Don't shy away. When life comes around to grab you, throw yourself out there. Just the colors in a room and people's faces, which are all treasure houses of impressions, can elevate you to states of mystic clarity. Watch even the nastiest person carefully enough, once or twice a week, and you'll have to be moved to compassion and tenderness.

You cannot let life consume you by a muscular effort of will. I have a fair degree of experience and I can't do it by an effort of will. I'm used to falling into it by default. You know how it is in car accidents—usually the people who are drunk don't get hurt because they are limp, mellow. The car goes over the cliff and they think, "Far out." They bounce when they hit because they're so relaxed. When you tense up that's when you break an arm or a leg. So cool out. Be gentle, easeful, melt into life. Let it wash over and through you like a sweet soft breeze.

Life is bigger than all the limitations we tend to put on it, and you need to be in an ongoing romance with life, otherwise it is easy to get buried by your own peculiar circumstances.

It's easy to become an automaton who gets up, works hard, even does spiritual practices, but all merely as a mechanical habit. You can easily get the idea that your spiritual work, or whatever you are doing, is all-important and that you must give your life to it, while at the same time you forget what "giving your life to it" actually means. Then you can become even more mechanical than you already are (if such a thing is conceivable), but in a different form.

The Work[13] wants your life—but only when you are in a love affair with life itself, only when you are bright, strong, confident, capable, in short: ALIVE. The Work does not want some kind of dull, dispassionate, struggling, agonizing humanoid. To give your life to the Work is to give breath and activity to the Work everyday; to give passion to the Work everyday. You have to have a childlike, eternal *beginner's mind*[14], a belief in miracles, like, "Any day anything can happen!"

To consider entering into an intimate relationship that could be for the rest of your life, and will most likely involve children (whether you want them or not), you've got to have this passionate kind of relationship to life. In a deep, and hopefully meaningful, commitment with another human being, when giving your lives to one another, you need to realize that life is bigger than your own intense little chamber. There will be times in which you are going to want to really tear into one another for some minor or even some imagined slight. There will be

---

13 Work, "The Work" - used in many spiritual traditions, and recently in the teachings of Gurdjieff, to refer to the Work of God in which human beings are called to participate. In Lee Lozowick's teaching it is synonymous with The Great Process of Divine Evolution and, as individuals, one's alignment with that. The Context of being moved by the Divine, and not by self-reference, determines whether any activity is the Work. The Work is objective *sadhana* (spiritual practice) and only one aligned to the Will of God can know what it is in any given moment.

14 beginner's mind - a descriptive term used by Shunryu Suzuki, Roshi, author of *Zen Mind, Beginner's Mind* (New York: Weatherhill, 1970) to mean approaching each moment as new. In the teaching of Lee Lozowick this is a mind which draws no conclusions about things *(Draw-No-Conclusions-Mind)*.

moments in which you think, "My God, I'm only forty. I've got another thirty years of this misery." You may think that it is absolutely impossible to make your relationship work. That's when you will most need to have this attitude of innocence—the belief that anything can happen. You've got to remember what LIFE is and always will be, no matter what your personal circumstances.

You can always access the largeness, the unlimitlessness of life, no matter how hopeless things appear. You don't get that by romancing your partner. You get that if you have a love affair with life itself—a passionate life. Then your relationships will be passionate and juicy too.

I recently listened to a radio interview with Henry Miller, one of my foremost heroes. He was eighty-five years old, with crippling arthritis, and he couldn't walk without a walker or even get out of bed without help. Still, the man's voice was just like his motto: "Always merry and bright." He said, "When you're my age you've got to consider sickness," and then he laughed. Practically every other sound out of his mouth was a laugh.

Now, here was Miller, unable to use the typewriter, barely able to see anymore (he was blind in one eye and half-blind in the other), so full of pain that he was up all night unable to sleep, yet still he was constantly full of passion, full of "spit and vinegar," as they say.

Miller said, "Americans don't like me, but the Europeans love me. I'm not popular in America." It's no wonder. Americans don't have any taste, one reason being that we let seeming problems dictate our moods and our opinions. We let circumstances define our relationships. If we don't get exactly what we want, when we want it, if we don't get exactly the food we want, if people aren't exactly the way we expect them to be, we get depressed or angry or abusive. You have to have a passionate fling with life to be bigger than such pettiness.

I've often discussed other alternatives, but it is entirely conceivable to me that we might only get one shot at life. So make it a wild, passionate fling! Make it real, total, rich, and full of possibility. Life should be a grand, majestic affair—the good, the bad, and the indifferent. If one day is a misery, be miserable. If you're "in the pits" one day, don't take it out on everybody else. Feel it, taste it, exude it. Don't bitch at your friends. If life is lousy one day, it will be great another day. That's beginner's mind. Anything could happen tomorrow. If for twenty years that is your attitude, and if for twenty years nothing does happen tomorrow, it doesn't matter. That attitude is enough!

If you don't have a love affair with life everyday, if you don't expect a miracle everyday, you're always going to be looking for God exclusively in what appears good—in the attractive, in the easeful, in the predictable. Most of you reading this are old enough and mature enough and have had enough experience to know that you should not expect appearances to convey everything. Appearances are totally subjective. Instead, you should look to the heart of things; feel through appearances to the Essence. Not only are you capable of that, you all do that naturally anyway. You just need to be aware that you do it, trust it, and make this awareness more real than the illusions of your trained beliefs and opinions. But you tend not to do that when the circumstances are making life look a little grey. "What's going to happen when the bill collectors start knocking on the door...?" you ask. And on and on.

You'll always have passion if you have *beginner's mind*. If your passion starts to die, it won't be because of your spiritual work, your friends, your lover, or because of life's down times. Your passion will die because you have bought—hook, line, and sinker—an attitude that was sold to you by your parents, your school teachers, and this society. You've bought the attitude that you've got to look like that *Playgirl* man (if you're a man) or that *Playboy* woman (if you're a woman). You think you've got to be cool and cultured, that you've got to dress right and smell like the corporate world wants you to smell. If your passion dies it will be because you've bought that appearances are everything, including the appearance of your worldview, politics, opinions, and beliefs.

To ultimately "make it" in this Work of Awakening, of Transformation, you have to embrace the miraculous—always. And that miracle is you being so much at peace with yourself that you can turn your energy towards welcoming and using the opportunities that are always falling into your lap. To embrace and devour these opportunities will make you free, happy, full of life, full of passion. Then your circumstances won't affect you so dramatically.

It is the nature of this Work that a revelation, a breakthrough, could happen at any time, and has many times! But, how easily we forget.

PART II

Sex—What it is and What it isn't

This section consists of simple, straight talk about the naturalness of human sexuality in an attempt to defuse an over-charged subject, and clarify some of the basic misunderstandings around sex.

Secret 10: Sex—Commodity or Communion?

Obviously there is an instinctual level of sexual activity which is to procreate. We are simply animals on that level, and the race must continue, so we are drawn to sex. But beyond that, in the modern world sex has become a commodity, and a very sophisticated and refined commodity. We live in a particular section of the world in which sex is not only just another commodity, but is probably *the* commodity. Obviously, in Bangladesh, or Cambodia and places like that, people have it and do it, but sex is not the be-all and end-all of life, as it is here. When refugees come to this country I'm sure they look at the T.V. ads and see that deodorant is given the place, in our culture, that rice is given in their culture. It's not deodorant in and of itself, but sexual attractiveness that's given such importance!

As we get closer to a truly disruptive world (and I don't mean just a lot of crime, I mean a really disruptive world) people are desperately looking for more and more and more. There is child sex and S&M and all of these things which we think are going to make us forget our human condition. But they don't. The moment after a fifteen second orgasm it's done, and you remember again. But that is how sex is subconsciously approached— to make us forget in a variety of ways.

We have grown up in a culture in which sex has been cheapened. If you look at the media and at advertising, any faint tendency towards Real sex is completely overridden by the neurotic need to copulate in a fashion that is consistent with the media hype that's been fed to us all our lives. There is a tremendous neurotic need in peoples' minds to copulate like a playgirl or a playboy, like a "swinger" or a "stud." Men's magazines, like *Playboy,* have been around for years, but *Playgirl* and other women's magazines are a relatively new phenomena. Actually, *Playgirl Magazine* isn't even the biggest offender. The biggest offenders are *Mademoiselle, Harper's Bazaar, Vogue, Cosmopolitan*—all the high-class "ladies" magazines. The articles in those magazines encourage the most unrealistic and superficial sexual and relational activity that one can imagine. They are not pornographic or particularly explicit, but they encourage women to be sappy, sentimental, bitchy, and adolescent. In the same way, in men's magazines men are encouraged to be tough when they need to be, understanding and tender when they need to be, and to know everything there is to know about women, sex, travel, cars, money, and food. Most of what goes down as sex today is simply a neurotic tendency to try and be who we've been trained to think we should be as men and as women.

These days there is no inherent sanctity to sex. A long time ago, in the most refined cultures of the world—ancient China, Japan, the Middle East, and India—the act of sex was given the most sacred consideration of any human act. The archetypal act of union was considered higher than eating, higher than dying, higher than birth. And, as is described in some of the old Indian treatises, for example, in each of those cultures the mundane sex act was always brought to a point of almost indescribable refinement. In Japan, only the strongest, most intelligent, creative, and disciplined women were trained in the many sophisticated arts necessary for *geishas.* In many countries of the Orient then, it was almost like the cream of the feminine crop were all courtesans, prostitutes, or *geishas.* Of course, among much of the population during those times there was also the common view of sex, which has always been the same...but within other more sophisticated circles there was great refinement. (And I'm not talking about the sophistication brought to sex by the Marquis de Sade. Obviously, there have been certain circles in which a different kind of sophistication was brought to the act of sex - one in which the more degrading you could be, the more sophisticated you were considered. And that still goes on today.)

Most of us, however, in the United States at least, grew up in an environment in which sex was hidden entirely. They didn't have programs like "Love Boat" and "Three's Company" on TV when we grew up. In my time they showed "sexless" married couples who slept in separate bedrooms and yet had gigantic families. If they didn't have separate bedrooms, at least their beds were completely separated, and they always slept fully dressed in nightclothes that only a puzzle-expert could get into or out of!

Even though the ordinary worldly influences that affected us as children were so totally charged with sexuality, adults were typically so insecure, confused, and scared of genuinely feeling sexuality that they superimposed a mood of asexuality on us. Without honesty and education, it's a wonder we didn't develop more strange superstitions about sex. (It's not that I think the comic-strip characters Sluggo and Nancy should be "doing it," but there is certainly a way of providing a valuable, honest education for children about sex.) In a culture devoid of sex, sex became a mystery, and we were therefore terrifed of it.

In my case, sex was a big mystery, and women or girls were unreachable. I never used the word "goddess" because I didn't think in those terms. Females were just unreachable, untouchable creatures—objects to lust after and dream about, but not to touch or even to talk to. We either grew up that way, or we grew up learning that sex should have no essential value at all. Perhaps our parents even talked about sex or about our neighbors in the most demeaning ways: "She's a whore, and I'm glad she's not my daughter." Sex has never been given its due value in our culture.

My opinion is that the act of sex should always be communion. Sex should be as significant as having a baby—profound, devotional, enrapturing. Obviously, that's an ideal. (I certainly don't expect that attitude to be prevalent even in a couple of generations in our Community, but that's the ideal I'm shooting for.) Sex is a sacred act, and should be treated as a sacred act every time, which doesn't mean you should only have sex twice a year either. The frequency is irrelevant. Whether sex is engaged every day, once a month, twice a month, or once a year, it is a sacred act. A conscious man or a conscious woman, someone with some real sensitivity, who is basically mature at the level of the third chakra (the sexual center) or above (at the level of the heart...etc.), holds within himself or herself the power for sex to be an entry or a doorway. That possibility should never be trampled upon. Union between a conscious man and a conscious woman is always sacred. And, admittedly, any consideration of sexuality, just like any consideration of spiritual life, will need to recognize the dilemmas and the problems that we face in this area.

These days sex is more like popping a candy bar in your mouth: there is no feeling, no depth, no usefulness. And orgasm isn't feeling! It's a little blip on the screen of energy. (But, that's enough for some people—"Hey, thank God I 'came,' now I can have a cigarette and go to sleep.")

Typically, unconscious people think that sex is just fun...that it feels good therefore they should do it whenever they get the chance. When I was in college I knew a bunch of guys who lived in a fancy singles' apartment building, with lots of airline stewardesses in apartments around them. They told me about the wild parties they would have and about how the stewardesses would sleep there if they got too drunk to leave. I found out that these guys never had sex with these women; they would

—
48

just sleep with them, and I couldn't believe it. As far as I was concerned, I would never get into bed with a woman if something wasn't going to happen! When I got a little older and had more experience, I developed a different idea about these things.

A lot of us, particularly the men, but even some of the women, are still like I was then—we want an immediate payoff with sex. We sense that there is something better down the road, but it's too chancey to wait for it. "What if I just sleep next to this woman all night and nothing happens? I'll have missed a night..." as if there isn't a next night and a next night and... We tend to think in very short terms. But, in this domain, that's not how things work. In this domain, what awaits the patient man or the patient woman is far, far greater than the immediate gratification. Because of the nature of sex, however, and because the immediate gratification can be so strong, we tend not to be willing to experiment. We have this unfortunate mentality—this attitude that there's no time.

Unconscious men usually feel that women should take care of birth control, and that they (the men) can always leave the relationship if the going gets tough. Unconscious women generally feel, "As long as I'm protected, well, what the hell?" The results of this unconsciousness are quite devastating, however. Just look at the incidence of herpes and the epidemic of venereal disease. These conditions are a kind of plague. It's not that there haven't always been venereal diseases, but in our day that's where the new plague shows up because we've essentially gone against the Law of God, which is the sanctity of the union between a conscious man and a conscious woman.

To consider the whole subject, of who we are as men and who we are as women, and to basically "clean up our acts," is very difficult because even if we are not promiscuous physically most of us are promiscuous in attitude. Flirtation predominates in almost all inter-gender relationships. Women flirt with men and men flirt with women when they are buying insurance or paying for groceries. This mood is pervasive in the culture and it creates a sickness worse than AIDS.

It is fairly easy to stay faithful physically—men have their work, women have things to occupy them. The common societal disease is that men come home from work at night too tired to have sex, and women are too hassled by the kids. Who has time or energy to consider the essential, objective fact that sex is a sacred ritual act?... To consider "As above, so below?"... To embody and act out the archetypal union of Shiva and Shakti during sex?

Actually, everything we do is an archetypal act, including eating and breathing. And sex is the most powerful archetypal, dualistic relationship in life. The act of sex is awesome when it unlocks the door to the domain of communion, which is literally the domain of creation. That doesn't mean procreation, which is the archetypal manifestation of the act of creation. Literally, the act of sex is the archetypal manifestation of what God did on the first day. Sex can be the key to that. Therefore, questions like, "Do I need to find a man or a woman right away and get in relationship and practice these things?" are all irrelevant if we haven't recognized and don't appreciate the principle concerning the sanctity of the act of sex.

That consideration of sanctity has to be the foundation for any apprenticeship to the body of knowledge that provides specific answers to all the questions regarding men and women. This is a vast, mysterious domain.

A man has to develop a different attitude towards a woman. Just the fact that a woman can get pregnant and have a baby is such an awesome mystery! It's not just a matter of tubes and ovaries—all that stuff we learned in biology. When I was sixteen, I called women "cows," and my female cousins would kick me and yell at me. But when I got to the point where I was really seeing what was going on, the mystery of it all was unspeakable. Women are really what's mysterious. Women are the Dharma[1]. Women are the Raw Divine. They have the potential to be spiritual energizers. (And men can learn to tap that energy and transform it to extend true Life, Beauty, and Reality outward on a larger scale.)

About men there's not so much mystery. Men are just Shiva. They are *just there!* They hunt and they bring back the goods. But women are very mysterious in an other-worldly sense. Until we all realize that, both men and women, then apprenticing to this body of knowledge is just like going to school anywhere else...it's useless. This body of knowledge about the transformational nature of sex is quite available, and easily communicable, but needs to be communicated on a certain foundation.

It is also not necessary to have a mate to engage this consideration even though at some point, obviously, it helps. What *is* necessary is to engage your own masculinity or your own femininity, and for men to engage the feminine aspect of themselves and for women to engage the masculine aspect of themselves. (And these subjects will be covered in later sections of this book.)

---

1 Dharma - the written or spoken Teaching of a spiritual Master; the philosophical argument of a spiritual Way; the objective spiritual teachings both traditional and contemporary. In specific usage it may be synonomous with the Truth, the Law, or Ultimate Reality.

Secret 11: Kaya Sadhana

Essentially, sexuality is non-problematical. It only becomes problematical when it becomes a means to an end rather than "just what it is" freely. The lineage that I'm associated with as a Teacher—the Bauls of Bengal—believes that the way to realization of God is *through* the body, not through denial or renunciation. This is called *Kaya Sadhana*. That means, that as long as we have a body it's a shame to waste good equipment…or let it rust or atrophy.

Don't deny your sexuality, therefore, and don't exaggerate, dramatize, or indulge it either. Allow your sexuality to respond naturally and spontaneously without artifice in relationship to the space, the mood, the circumstance, and the environment. Sexuality is not a law unto itself. It doesn't make its own rules irrespective of every other factor in the environment (although our minds act as if it should). In other words, when the "heat is on," it doesn't mean you've got to hop on the nearest person of the opposite sex (or the same sex, if that's your disposition)…or on the nearest goose.

Secret 12: Genuine Sex Education

When most people think of the word "sex" they think of copulation, not Life. They think of what happens for a specific period of time with specific physical organs, (possibly including a little foreplay and afterplay), and they limit sex to that.

With my students I do not often speak in detail about specific sexual practices. We have talked generally about an approach to sex, but I have stayed away from specific instruction in Taoist, Buddhist, or Hindu tantric technology. One of the reasons is that the joining of man and woman in genuine sexual communion doesn't need instruction. Academically, if our lives were surrendered to the essential Work we were doing, if our lives were free of the handicap of the cramp, if our lives were not defined by the strategy of survival, the highest forms of sexual communion would flow very naturally from within our relationship as a couple. No instruction would be necessary.

A few years ago there were two books that were very popular for awhile—one on the use of male sexual energy and one on the use of female sexual energy. Everyone was reading them and getting excited about all the techniques. One of the men in our community was reading the book on female sexuality, and another man asked him about why he was reading that one instead of the one for men. He said something like, "I've learned more from reading this book than I have in years of studying women."

It struck me again how easily seduced we are by techniques, and how unwilling we often are to learn from life itself. That person thought that all of the descriptions of techniques *meant* something. But the techniques are cool, unreal, mental. It's true that if you read those books and use the techniques you can get a pretty strong buzz on, but that's not the point. A man doesn't need books on sexual energy if all he wants to do is have a bunch of women think he is the best screw they ever had. On the other hand, if a man or a woman is really interested in what sexual energy is and what it means, all those techniques don't amount to much. That is because the use of them will only make you an energy-mechanic-machine. You will be able to manipulate energy very effectively, even brilliantly, and 99% of the people on whom you manipulate it will be wildly impressed. But none of that has anything to do with the transformational possibilities of sex as I'm speaking of it in this book, or with what we are doing in spiritual work together. You can experiment with those kinds of things here and there if you don't miss the point. But, essentially it's all missing the point.

You don't need to know which muscles to clamp, when to breathe in and when to breathe out, when to cross your eyes, and when to put your hands around your partner's neck. You don't need to read the *Kama Sutra* or the *Ananda Rang* or *The Perfumed Garden*.

Can you imagine two Bauls getting ready to have sex—sitting in front of one another and looking into one another's eyes to get into the mood? No way! When Bauls are ready to do it, they do it. They tackle one another. They go for it. Passion! There is none of this cool shit, none of this working up to it…none of this staying away from one another, as some Tantric books recommend. If they want to caress, they get in there and caress. They use their hands, their feet, their ears, anything they can use. They don't watch every breath and every thought as the man enters the woman. None of that stuff.

Sex has got to be natural. If you're going to do tantra, it should be spontaneous, natural tantra; and if you love someone deeply enough you will do tantra. The kind of conventional "getting your rocks off" attitude that exists around sex is a function of selfishness. If you are not selfish and your own satisfaction doesn't come first, even if there are subconscious drives, you will discover tantra naturally in your intimate relationships, and in relationships with friends also. Tantra works between friends. You will discover it naturally if you are not selfish in a relationship, although it might take a little while.

What you need is for your life to be free of the strategy of survival[2], in every moment. Then, sexual communion will be the most natural expression of bonded love between mates. "Sex Education" from my viewpoint is essentially about working with denial, confusion, unconsciousness, the cramp, recoil, reactivity—whatever you call it. If you clear up the obstacles in that domain, you don't need sex education. The essential urge to join in communion and travel through the labyrinth of love between man and woman is completely instinctual. It needs no training. Man and woman, as polarities in the great universal scheme of things, actually know the way through that labyrinth. You will know the way when nothing stands in between your knowledge (which I refer to as Organic Innocence[3]), and your journeying. All the things that do stand in between are the things that you need to work on.

So, to train yourself in esoteric sexual techniques, in the manipulation of body systems, is putting the cart before the

---

2 strategy for survival - the vast repertoire of ego's attempts to survive as a separate, independent entity, all of which keep one under the illusion of separation from God.

3 Organic Innocence - a term which characterizes the basic ground of being of all existence; the essential intelligence of being or existence itself as it shows up in particularized forms. For human beings, to function "from Organic Innocence" means to live as the body, because "the body knows," intuitively.

horse. When you have hooked the horse up properly, that's all you need to do. To understand intention is far, far more important than any consideration of specific techniques—of how to do anything. Sexual energy is alive in life, in being in relationship. Techniques like those in books depersonalize. They turn life into business, genitals into tools, people into mechanics or computer operators. The use of techniques by "sleeping man"[4] doesn't help to wake him, but serves to reinforce the principles upon which sleep or habit arises and is sustained. That is very dangerous to one's work.

We don't have to train ourselves. The only thing we have to do is remove the obstacles superimposed upon us as essential beings. When the things we are working on are practiced free of complication and confusion, we *will be* sensual beings when we need to be. We will be in sexual communion with our partner when that's called for. We will also, in fact, be in sexual communion with nature. No one, no malevolent spirit, has superimposed these things on us. The human condition is the human condition.

The human condition gives us certain challenges, and when we have successfully met those challenges, the rest of it is pure instinct.

The primary challenge, of course, is resolving the strategy of survival so that it ceases to be the autonomous governing factor in our moment-to-moment functioning. You don't follow instinct with your mind. Following instinct is not a matter of seeing signposts ahead of you and knowing which way to go.

Following instinct means being "what is wanted and needed in the moment," that is, being in alignment with the Will of God.

That's all there is to it.

---

4   sleeping man - terminology used by Gurdjieff and others to indicate the condition of the unconscious human who has not yet awakened to his work function, or realized his essential condition as being non-separate from God.

Secret 13: A Good Orgasm is Never the End of The Road, Although Sometimes It's a Detour

Most people close their eyes when they are having sex because they think that what's really going on is happening between their legs. Actually, whatever we've got between our legs is the starting place only. Genital pleasure is almost irrelevant. Tantric sexual work is not about how your genitals feel when you're coupled. If you need to couple in that way to begin something, you do, but that is just starting the snowball rolling down the hill. Most people have a good orgasm and think that is the avalanche. If you are a man, an orgasm is the ridge that stopped the snowball before it could do any real damage. If you are a woman, a good orgasm is just another gateway.

But an orgasm is never the end of the road. Sometimes it's a detour. We should just smash through the detour, tear down the barricades and keep going over the cliff. When you go over the cliff, it's not because your genitals are coupling. It's an Alchemical process that touches and affects every aspect of being, even the subtle ones.

Actually, there is more happening in the eyes than in the genitals. But most of us don't want to look in someone's eyes when we are really sexing, because if we do, we will forget about our genitals. The eyes will draw us like a whirlpool, into a deep and endless cavern, holding every treasure, every discovery, all possibility. And we will most definitely not remember something as pitifully insignificant as a "dick" or a "cunt" when we are expanding our being into infinite space and consciousness, into Light and Revelation.

—

Secret 14: Sex for Men; Sex for Women

A fantastic one-page editorial appeared in *Playboy Magazine* recently. It was about how a man and woman can make love, and how this lovemaking can be beautiful, elevating, extraordinary, even cosmic. When it's over, however, the man lies back, smiling, and the woman says (and these are not direct quotes), "Is that all?" He says, "What?" And she says "You never talk to me." He says, "I thought we just had this beautiful moment of communion." She says, "Sex is not all there is to life." And he says, "But it wasn't *just sex*. I love you. It was beautiful. It was great." And she says, "We never talk!"

So the guy says, "What did I do wrong? I took my time. We made love for two hours. I was sensitive to every one of your feelings and your thoughts. I was responsive." But she says, "Yes, but it was *sex*." The guy says, "What's wrong with *sex*?" For men—even for a man who is sensitive, considerate, and understanding (as much as a man can be)—a pivotal aspect of relationship is sex.

The writer ends the editorial by asking when women are going to understand that to a woman a relationship is sex...and talk... and comfort...and affection, and to a man it's sex? It doesn't mean the man doesn't love the woman. (The man loves the woman at least as much as the woman loves him.) But to him, a sensitive night of lovemaking is enough. He doesn't need to talk. He doesn't need to rehash the obvious in a verbal mode. He doesn't need to process, to psychologize, to socialize, to philosophize. To a man all of these are covered by and included in the field of touch, taste, smell and feeling that lovemaking encompasses.

Does this sound like the rhetoric that women use when they criticize what is lacking in men? You bet it does! Does something seem amiss? You bet it is! What? Oh...

And, yes, men do have the need to share their innermost feelings. The writer said that when the man has an orgasm, that *is* sharing his deepest innermost feelings. There is nothing else to share. (Of course, as I will elaborate later on, ejaculatory conservation produces a whole different, more intense and more vulnerable sharing of innermost feelings. But the example is clear.)

When the woman says, "Let's talk about it," she wants to dissect it, to re-enter it from many angles. "You don't understand me," she moans when the man looks frustrated.

We men understand perfectly. It's just that what life is to the man is different. He offers his innermost soul through tactile and sensual communication...and when it's done, it's done.

Secret 15: Sexual Experimentation
Within Relationship

There are three stages to sexual practice—infatuation, sexual experimentation, and finally tantric sex, or sexual communion.

In the first stage: just get together, love each other, be friends, develop a peaceful relationship that is full of gentleness and concern and service. That's all, for however long it takes. Have deep enjoyment and affection for one another, free of violence—physical and emotional, psychic and astral. Just be simple and "together."

Love doesn't develop because of sex alone, but sexual communion is both an enticement towards love, and the effective result of love. The sex drive awakens because of infatuation. You don't merely see someone and that's it—"Oh my God, I'm in love." You see someone...you're infaturated...sex happens ...and then, out of that, love can grow.

The second stage is sexual experimentation. By the second stage, you are committed to the relationship. You are really together, and could even say that you love one another. The infatuation might still be there, but it's deepened to the point where it isn't airy and blindly unrealistic. You're grounded and committed. Sex may not happen as often as or exactly how you would like, but it's pretty good. It's satisfying, if not perfect.

In this second stage you pull the fantasies out of the closet. It's not that you dive into every kinky variation imaginable, act out all your fantasies, or talk about them all. The worst thing that could happen is that you have no secrets from one another. Share your hearts, don't share you minds. (What trash the mind is full of!) Bare you soul, absolutely, but not your mind. "Well, it's truth night. You know, I really love you, don't take this wrong, but sometimes when we're having sex, I fantasize that you're Paul Newman..." Don't ever do that, because it's all shit! Your mind is a cesspool. Bare your soul, open your hearts and your "vitals"[5] to one another, bond together, but basically, leave your mind shut.

In this second stage you air your pockets of resistance, poison, and repression, not necessarily to one another, but you free yourself of conditioned and biased limitations. Maybe you consider orgasm together in a different way. You might seriously consider together different energetic approaches, an entirely different viewpoint towards sex—perhaps the viewpoint of "sex from God" instead of "God from sex."

In sexual experimentation you may make love for longer periods of time, or shorter periods of time. Sometimes forty-five minutes will be the perfect amount of time. At other times neither party will be satisfied after those forty-five minutes. (You can get a physical satisfaction, an immediate kind of buzz, in only ten minutes, but there is also a deeper satisfaction that is possible in sex.) Sometimes two hours is the right time... sometimes five hours! (That doesn't happen very often, just every once in a while.)

Some people like to consider themselves sexual athletes, and they aren't satisfied unless they've had sex for three hours every time. The implication in some Taoist books is that whenever you make love it should be for three to four hours, and that the more you learn the techniques, the more you'll make love all

---

5   vitals - referring to the vital center, i.e. the "gut" or the moving center (in 4th Way or Gurdjieffian terminology) from which movement is generated.

day, and for days at a time. But, that isn't true. That's ego—an intellectual concept about how long you have to go. And it's exactly the same dynamic you've always had—towards success, fame, power, or possessions—except that it's more powerful and more elevating. The end result will not be what you are looking for, even though you might think it is because such extended sex makes you feel so much more siginificant than anything else has made you feel. (Except listening to Jim Morrison and the Doors, of course.)

If you are responsive to the mood of two people making love, there is essentially no set time. You work with each other until there is a feeling between both of you that you have reached a certain sexual point at which continuing would be redundant. One thing about redundancy, beyond what it does to a mood, is that it really tends to confuse the issue, and that is something you don't want to do if you are attempting to work with sexual energy. Sex is a domain in which the issue can be confused enough as it is. So you need to be sensitive.

When you "hit" something good, you will know it. There might be a little voice in your head that will say, "Got it! Now it's working. This is what I've paid my dues for." That's well and good. But, the tendency then is not to want to stop it at the right time. You want to milk the experience for everything it's worth, because who knows whether you will be able to reach this point again next time. But you also need to have a little voice that says, "Perfect. Time to stop." You need to be very, very sensitive.

In this second stage of sexual experimentation you may make love in different ways, or free of the usual demands and expectations. You essentially clear the obstructions to your sexual lives. A lot of people think they have done that in the first stage, but my experience has been that there are certain things that are taboo in the first stage—because you're scared of "rocking the boat." (I've seen more than one self-styled macho male turn as pale as death because the woman said, "Spank me.")

62

In the second stage the relationship is solid—you know you love one another so you don't have to be worried about saying or doing the wrong thing and ruining the relationship. You don't have to be worried about sticking it in her ear and having her say, "I want a divorce." If you make a mistake, you make a mistake, that's all. She simply says, "It's not my style," and you say, "Okay," and you're still friends. So, in the second stage you clear the obstructions to a completely free sexual dynamic, and you settle on your sexual preferences—the healthy ones and those that support your practice and your devotional orientation towards the Divine.

By the second stage you will be honest and mature enough with one another so that the unhealthy sexual preferences can be cleared out. (And I would call being roped onto a cross and whipped senseless an unhealthy one. It's not common, but it's definitely not rare either.) Unhealthy sexual preferences are not sexual preferences, but neurotic dependencies. In the second stage, you clear that stuff out. The sunlight of self-honesty dries them up, purifies neurotic patterns and distractions. You don't necessarily play them out by doing them, that's a good way to seduce yourself into a dead end, and an unhealthy one at that. You transcend your neurotic dependencies through clarity and right practice.

The third stage is a stage of tantric sex, regenerative sex, or sexual communion, in which you consider conservation of orgasm experientially and, eventually, the effects that such sexual communion produces in the Mind-Body-Being. It's not that you won't do this in the first and second stages, but it becomes a natural practice of your lives together in the third stage—beyond a mere consideration.

Most people do sex degeneratively. They use orgasm for a release of neurotic tension, which expends any kind of built up tension that they might have stored for doing spiritual or transformational work. Regenerative sex honors the profound energetic possibility of sex. You can get a tremendous "edge" from those tensions, i.e. you can use those tensions as fuel instead of screwing them away and getting rid of them all. You should go into sex high and come out of it higher—not go into it low and come out of it relieved.

Regenerative sexuality, however, is of no value if everything else that you do is degenerative. Some dietary health supplements are great, but if you expect them to clear your body out, when all the while you drink, smoke and eat poison, why bother? Life itself should be regenerative. You should be singing the praises of God bodily, emotionally, physically and energetically, all the time. Sex can be regenerative if you chant, enjoy life, are happy with people, exercise, and eat the appropriate foods. If you are trying to do tantra as an excuse for having sex, and the rest of your life is degenerative, nothing will ever happen— except that you'll have lots of sex. But, nothing useful will ever happen.

Sexuality should not be used as a hold on someone, as in: "I own you a little bit now, but after we screw I'm going to own you a lot." That is really immature. Sexuality should be expressed in relationship between two people as the fullness of their lives together in God, not as another "noose"—as you see in the typical comedy "schtick" about a woman going on a sex strike, locking the bedroom door if she's angry at her husband. That might look like "winning," from the woman's viewpoint, but it's actually using what should be a prayer to the Goddess[6] (both for men and women), for petty and egoistic purposes. Using sex as a bargaining point is outrageous. It's not good or bad. It just shows that we're immature. Sexuality should be a matter of fullness, not a matter of contraction, between individuals.

---

6   Goddess - Manifestation; the Creation; the feminine aspect of the Divine; the impersonal Feminine; also may refer to particular female deities.

Secret 16: Managing Sexual Energy

A student recently asked me how to conserve his sexual energy. "I don't know what to do with it. I'm getting a little crazy and foaming at the mouth," he joked.

Well, there are a number of ways of dealing with sexual energy. Up to a certain point, you can just keep it in the body. Just keep it in the body and you will soon feel like Muhammed Ali. That ain't so bad. You'll feel great—full of vitality. A little bit beyond that, however, and you might start feeling "wired," and then "foaming at the mouth," as the student said.

Of course, just having a lot of sex, with no conservation of energy, will take the pressure off—release it immediately. Other than that, however, there are four things you can do with strong sexual energy—two of which I recommend and two of which I don't. The two that I recommend are hard work or some form of art. Either is fine. Of the other two options, which I don't recommend, one is negativity—complaining, arguing, a good fight. (Any form of psychic or verbal violence gets rid of built up sexual energy, or ceases to conserve it.) And the fourth approach is to move the energy up and out of the body into the higher chakra system. If that is the option you choose there are a lot of metaphysical programs for training in connecting the chakra[7] system in the physical body to a higher chakra system. My

---

7   chakras - points or places of energy accumulation or focus within the subtle energy system of the body. Different systems of thought (Hindu, Taoist) designate differing numbers of such energy centers.

dislike of that option, however, is based in principle on the fact that the mind making the decision to circulate the energy in relationship to a higher source is the same thing as ego defining how our lives work. (It's certainly better than violence, but not as good as maintaining a balance within the body or working hard.)

My own experience about conservation of energy is that if you engage a relatively active sexual life without ever having ejaculatory orgasm, you had better have a lot of hard work or be one hell of an artist, or basically you'll be uncomfortable a lot. That transformation of sexual energy is a process that you go into over time, and in the meantime, I recommend that you have other fairly healthy forms of release. Just maintain balance and don't become too rigid about this practice.

Creativity and good work seem to be the best ways to manage sexual energy. It's amazing what a day of work in the garden will do. I don't ride horses, but I would guess that a two-hour horseback ride would do wonders for "taking the edge off," if you don't know what else to do with the sexual energy. Working with other life forms (other than human) is a tremendously effective way to balance the energy. Then, rather than doing something artificial to maintain balance or release excess energy, the body is in a natural orientation to the energy dynamic. Over time, your nervous system becomes able to hold a higher charge. Over time you build your capacity for current.

Secret 17: When Sex Is Lovemaking

Lovemaking is not just sex. It can be anything. Some people make love with their cooking, or by taking an engine of a car apart. Lovemaking doesn't have to take place only in an artistic domain.

Typically, one *falls* into lovemaking, almost accidentally—like all of a sudden you stumble upon a whole different possibility for what lovemaking can be. But as long as the mind stays fixed in its usual rigid patterns, there's no other possibility for lovemaking. There's no possibility if a man is always thinking, "How long can I have sex? How many times can I experience the woman's orgasm? I better do this right or she won't love me." Women think other thoughts. As long as one's mind is doing that, lovemaking doesn't show up. Certainly there might be a very intense passionate experience, but that's not necessarily lovemaking. So, it's important not to identify lovemaking with the degree of heightened intensity, because we can have extraordinary heightened intensity and not have lovemaking; and we can have almost no intensity and have lovemaking.

You can be lovemaking in the kitchen, chopping vegetables. It doesn't mean you'll be twirling around, whipping the knife in the air and singing arias. Quite the contrary. You might be sitting very calmly. Anyone else might look at you and think, "Boy, what a dull carrot-chopper." You don't need to have an extraordinary, physical manifestation of energy. Lovemaking, as I'm speaking of it here, could be literally unnoticable to an external viewer.

Secret 18: Sexual Fantasy—It's Not What It Seems

In the whole process of sex it is not necessary (if even possible) to stop having fantasies. The way to deal with fantasy, however, is not to blithely concede its existence or to try to forcibly subdue it. The first thing to do is to recognize that the fantasy is real, or rather that it has its own reality. It *did* actually arise. That's the foundation key—to genuinely see that fantasy has a reality of its own, and not to intellectualize or minimize your observation.

When you can accept and acknowledge your fantasy as having a reality, it becomes as if it already happened. In that case, any physical need to act out the fantasy becomes quite unnecessary, irrelevant actually, because to the mind (which is so easily fooled, even by itself) the deed has happened and is already history. (Of course, in the fancy non-dualistic sphere of things there is never the thought, "I wonder what it would be like..." In complete non-duality there is an absolute *knowing* what it already was like because it already *was*—and it was all an illusion. Each thing is only what it is and no more.) It's the projections beyond what anything *is* that get us in trouble.

Life is sex, money, food, breath, ego, emotions. Life is incarnation. Life is not getting away from who we are as a manifest form of existence. Life is not about retiring to the subtle realms, it's about this realm. No one who wakes up in the morning, opens their eyes, looks in the mirror, goes to pee, can seriously think that they are not *here*. Imagining that we are somewhere else is clinical insanity.

We all eventually have to confront life as it is and deal with it directly. There are certain things that are always appropriate and there are certain things that are not appropriate. (It's obvious what is not appropriate because these things are always forms of physical, psychic, or emotional abuse.) Our job then is not to stop having fantasies or separate realities, but rather to cease to be under a cloud of blindness and delusion, to get beyond the myriad levels and veils of denial. So, if your sexual fantasy with your partner is along the lines of, "It's not happening here, and I wish it would happen somewhere else," this will need to be confronted and dealt with. This is a form of blindness.

Recognize that the fantasy is a separate reality and do not try to force it into or project it upon this reality. When we try to make our fantasies this reality, that is where all the problems arise. That is where people get more deeply rooted in disease, in the illusions of incompleteness and discomfort.

• • •

When you are in a relationship with someone and you love them, you are certainly going to notice attractive people of the opposite sex, but that noticing doesn't need to interfere with the relationship. Only if you indulge this attraction will it interfere. Then, all of a sudden, you start fantasizing, finding fault with your mate, wondering how other people would be in bed …Then the relationship starts to break down. If fantasy is simply stream-of-consciousness with no attention, nothing happens. There is no distraction. What makes something a distraction is when your attention is moved to it, taken, or hooked by it. What makes something a distraction is when you give your attention and energy to it willingly and intentionally (albeit unconsciously). A distraction is when your attention is taken. A seduction is when your attention and energy are given. If you don't break attention, you have no distraction and no fantasy. Period.

Whenever you notice that you are being sexually distracted by someone other than your mate, return your attention to your mate; that will reinforce your ability to not be distracted and not be seduced. Keep your attention on your work when you're working, on your mate when you're mating, on whatever your particular job is in the moment. It's very simple and very basic. The strength of your effective attention becomes a source of "food."

It's not a matter of overriding the attraction. Rather, it's about replacing it. You can only do two things with attention—either it's *On* or it's *Off*. If you leave it *On* what you are attracted to, you will be distracted and seduced. If you take it *Off* what you are attracted to, you haven't sublimated or avoided it, you have simply placed your attention somewhere else. That is a very important distinction.

Sometimes, because of the way the mind works, we don't even realize right away that we are distracted, or not paying attention. That's why the Work doesn't happen overnight. That's why after ten years we're just getting our teeth into it...a little bit.

Secret 19: If You Don't Have a Partner... and even if you do...

How do you consider real intimacy without a lover?

Consider intimate relationship with friends, children, and family, simply without the use of sexual play or engagement. Such relationships don't mean that you have no sexual energy, but (hopefully) these relationships will just not elicit the same response as a lover or mate would. If you're able to be a friend successfully, and manage your sexual energy effectively and maturely, then you're probably ready to use sexual energy in a transformative and alchemical way within the confines of a lovers' relationship. If you're not able to do that successfully, then before you begin the esoteric use of sexual energy you should "get it together" first (grow into the maturity of adult values and ethic) and be prepared to live without a love relationship until you can serve one correctly and maturely.

It is not productive to build up a lot of sexual tension and then, in an emotional fury, end up jumping into a relationship that doesn't serve your higher needs and desires. You may get heat flashes once in awhile, but if you can wait for a relationship that serves, that's a very important sign of what goes on in all areas of your life, and therefore of the possibility of higher alchemy.

Be vulnerable to people, so when a love relationship comes along you don't constrict in the way we tend to constrict ordinary relationships.

Within my community, if someone is outside of a committed love relationship, but essentially open to one, the basic conditions of spiritual practice are all the same—study, meditation, exercise, vegetarian diet, and so on. The considerations of the purification of the lower dimensions (lower centers or chakras), the maturity of the descending process of *prana/shakti,* are also relatively the same, as are the considerations of the higher dimensions, of the transformation of the effects of the ascending channels (See Secret 50).

At higher levels of practice there are ways of utilizing and transforming sexual energy that have to do with working with breath. By breath I mean the literal process of breathing which includes both the use of oxygen and musculature, and also the use of *prana* or life force (*ki* or *chi*). Thus, in principle, there are ways of using sexual energy internally when one doesn't have a partner. With a partner the effects are also internal, but essentially you learn to use the external contact to facilitate the internal effect.

Although I will have more to say about this subject in later sections of the book, I'm hesitant to describe the precise utilizations of energy because there are refinements that depend on a person's exact makeup and this can only be judged by direct personal interaction. In matters of such delicacy one should have a teacher or guru and not just begin using techniques from a book.

Secret 20: Sex Beyond Limits

All alchemy is provocative. Consequently, we may be afraid of what invention[8] in the domain of sex—of doing what has never been done before (I'm not talking about anything kinky or dangerous to the physical organism)—will provoke. We may be so crystallized in certain habit patterns that we cannot allow other options to arise.

To fear the domain of possibility[9] in sex is to almost guarantee that the "food" that will be provided for one another within a couple will be seriously limited. Or it might mean that there will be disintegration within the couple which will eventually destroy the relationship.

Invention is terrifying because it is unknown. In sex we want everything to be known. A woman wants affection and tenderness. A man wants to dominate. All very defined. For instance, some men are very easily satisfied (until next time) simply by a certain disposition in the woman, or by an orgasm. Some women are satisifed by hearing, "I love you." They don't care

---

8 invention - term adapted by Werner Erhard to describe the creation of something new, something that "wasn't supposed to happen," something that could only occur if the individual had made a leap outside of the normal, limiting definitions of the nature of reality. Activity that is Organically Innocent, not based on linear, mental, cause-and-effect relationship.

9 domain of possibility - used by Werner Erhard to describe a state of existence outside of the normal, limiting definitions of reality within which most humans live. When one is operating from, or living in, the domain of possibility, invention is the norm.

how violent, ugly or brutal the sex is, as long as the man says the right thing. Therefore, if one approaches sex with an easily satisfiable goal, out of fear the tendency will be to absolutely reject, fight, and resist the domain of possibility within sexual communion. To enter into the domain of possibility and feel that the act of sex could literally lead to being blasted into infinity, so that one might never come back, is so terrifying that many people feel the approach of invention and immediately put a cap on their sexual activity. Even if they have sex four times a day, they will not allow it to go beyond a certain point.

Invention, in a practical sense, is when you have redefined the matrix of your being. When you bring the context of the domain of possibility to sex, therefore, it becomes an arena in which such invention is highly probable. Statistically, invention is a lot more likely to happen in sex than in sharing a hamburger with somebody. It's not more possible, but it is more likely. Being "backed up against the wall" is another arena in which invention is more likely. When you've got lots of options, nothing is going on—you've done your spiritual practices for the day, and you just want to hang out and chat. In that case, the likelihood of invention is minimal. When you are "backed up against the wall," however, with no options, you must face yourself and your resistance.

For most people, the inability to access the domain of possibility is because they try to view this domain through the definition of form. But the domain of possibility can't be defined that way.

A sexual relationship needs to be contextualized by approaching it from the domain of possibility. Keeping sex within the bounds of love is fine, but also: "Sex is sex, and love is love." They may show up together, but they are not the same thing. Sex is essentially an energetic process, and love is not. Love transcends energetic processes. Love can alchemetize the energy of the process, but sex is not love and we shouldn't mistake the two. Sex may be a wonderful element of love, but sex itself is not love. For ordinary human love to be present there has to be an ego. But the definition of S*E*X is - "Suddenly Ego EXits." For ordinary human love, there has to be an object and a subject, and when "suddenly ego exits" there is no subject and object. That's Real Sex!

When you approach sex from the domain of possibility, the responsibility for the energetic play that can happen is yielded to the intelligence of the energy. The energy has innate intelligence. The body knows!

To rest in the context of the domain of possibility during sex allows the energy of the interaction its own process. The energy will never overstress someone—will never produce alchemy that would destroy the people in the couple. The energy is ultimately intelligent. Simply let the energy be what it is in sex. If we are thinking about *how* it should be, then what we have is an *attempt to invent,* but with a definition of limitations already. You are saying, "I want invention, but it has to be like this." If you rest in the domain of possibility, the energy will be the guiding intelligence—not ego, not your cramp, psychology, relationship to men, women or pleasure. The energy will define what happens.

When the energy defines what happens, it blows all the limitations off the possibility of the sexual event. "Does that mean I'll have fifty orgasms instead of three?... Oh, will there be more intense pleasure than I've ever known?..." Any definition limits the possibility of invention. You cannot define invention. You simply have to approach sex from the domain of possibility, and what that produces can be very threatening.

For instance, within a relationship, possessiveness, exclusiveness and jealousy often arise. Functioning in the domain of possibility would be so threatening to those limitations that, were sex to be the stimulus for that state of consciousness (the domain of possibility) arising in someone, it is likely that his or her partner would never approach sex from the same place again. Sex like that would never be allowed to happen again, because the threat of that kind of freedom would be too great.

If a man falls into the domain of possibility during sex it doesn't mean he will start eyeing every woman he sees. It means that maybe for the first time in his mate's life the woman will know what receiving adoration is; and it will be real Adoration (see Secret 63) not just his saying, "I love you, I love you."

Invention can mean anything. It can even mean that one of the people in the sexual relationship will be thrust into a domain of such intensity that he or she can't have sex—that sex literally becomes almost poisonous for them, from a non-neurotic position. (It's just neurotic bullshit if one of the people says, "I don't want sex because I need to be pure for God.") What happens to the other partner? Hey, they're stuck with no sex. That's the deal they make when as a couple they approach the Divine together. What do they do when they get really horny, when they're climbing the walls? They raise their focus beyond the level at which sex is the only thing that will bring the body to the point of resolution. They do what Anandamayi Ma's[10] husband did—become a devotee. Then, what they give instead of sex is adoration. What they take instead of sex is adoration. Within the domain of possibility, anything can happen.

When one is really feeling sexual it feels like the only resolution is sexual resolution. But that's not true. Actually there are a lot of things that can bring the body to a point of balance, but we have not been trained to do that. We are not trained to work with energetic systems. We are trained to satisfy desires at the point of desire—when the stomach wants something, we eat; when the genitals want something, we sex; when the head wants something, we sleep—rather than transmute the desire

---

10 Anandamayi Ma - a renowned Indian saint who remained celibate for her entire life.

into a satisfiable domain. (Of course, if a lot of us were able to take our sexual frustrations and put them into our stomachs we would be 270 pounds within a short matter of time!)

If you suppress the domain of possibility in sex you take the chance of suppressing a lot more. If you do not suppress the domain of possibility in sex, ego takes the chance of losing a lot. So, some big sacrifices may be in order.

Often invention shatters us. Perhaps we have this whole idea of family life, but then invention happens and it may all be shattered. So the question becomes, do we pick up the pieces, take invention as the foundation in our lives and go from there ...or do we try to put together the broken pieces and re-structure the old foundation?

I say go into the shattering! It is not possible to have the old foundation back except from a different context.

PART III

Building Love

This group of profound secrets deal with the common, conventional definitions of love, explaining why these are inadequate and even damaging. Mr. Lee offers a description of conscious love, explaining the steps and processes which allow such love to grow within a relationship. This section serves as an introduction to Tantric practice.

Secret 21: Start With Friendship

You shouldn't couple up with someone if you are not friends. Whenever intimate relationships break up, including friendships, I always experience a good deal of sorrow because good friends are much harder to find than good lovers. I wouldn't want a lover who wasn't a friend, and if you are smart you wouldn't either. Love begins with chemistry, and if love stays and if you're lucky it gets to the heart. You can always manage chemistry somehow, but you can't always manage the heart, and friendship has to do with the heart—real friendship is a heartful matter, from beginning to end.

You know the saying, "Old friends are gold and new ones silver or copper." But we have a tendency to take for granted our friendships with one another, and then, when flashy new people show up with their predictable seductions, we so easily shift alliances (of course with very rational justifications).

Friendship is not a matter of some exclusive and isolated circumstance. You can be good friends with twenty people, all at the same time, not play favorites, and still maintain integrity. When you give yourself to someone as a friend, it's for life. That is the way real friendships should be in any case—for life. Even if your friend gets "bummed out" and never wants to see you again, that is their dynamic, their problem. It doesn't change your friendship one bit.

In intersex communications, for instance, there are those times when people's eyes meet and they are sure they are "soul-

---

mates" or that they have unfinished karmic business between them. But typically, real love between a man and a woman who could become a couple grows over time through friendship and attention.

Often, our initial response to someone may be a function of our own need systems and chemistry at the moment. If we approach as friends, however, instead of as business associates ("I'll give you praise if you give me sex, etc...") something more can grow from that.

Friendship is always a good place to start.

Secret 22: Honor In Relationship

By the time you've finished reading this book most of you will well know that the word *love* is something I probably couldn't be cynical enough of. I've tried often enough to replace it with refined and sophisticated synonyms—life, reality, truth, suffering—but nothing exactly equals it to my satisfaction. Yet, I still resist using that word, mightily, both based on the unconscious psychological mechanisms triggered by it and on the fact that it is so easily misunderstood in the conscious vein.

Listen to how often "I love you" is spoken, and then ask yourself, "Is there honor in all of these relationships?" Is what that phrase means honored in practice, in action, and even in deep thought, not just between lovers, but between parents and children also? How many parents say "I love you" to their children, yet have no honor or respect in the relationship? Often, the same children they say "I love you" to are also beaten, molested, shamed and neglected. There must be honor in relationships for any kind of integrity or beauty in life.

You probably have friends who are divorced and desperate for relationship, yet they don't have any integrity in their relationships. For example, as much as they say they love their children, when they meet somebody of the opposite sex who looks good enough, they are gone, and the kid is left alone or sloughed off to some babysitter. They think to themselves, "I'll make it up to my kids later. I've got to leap on this opportunity now."

If the person you are dating is willing to have you do that, they ain't much of an opportunity (which I'm sure some of you have found out).

In the Western world "I love you" is probably said billions of times a day, but how much honor is held and conveyed in action behind these words? How much integrity is there? Most people don't even have the common sense to say, "Well, I'm shallow and self-centered, but I'd *like* to be able to sacrifice to my circumstance with some depth, integrity and honor."

In my own life it took me a long time to even start thinking about honor. But that's what we need to come to. No amount of discipline replaces honor.

Secret 23: Beware the Cult of Pairs

I once knew a couple who used to go everywhere together. They could barely be separate even to go to the bathroom! It was a 24-hour-a-day, 7-day-a-week, 31-day-a-month affair. If she had an appointment or an interview, he would go with her. If he had an appointment or an interview, she would go with him. Theirs was a compulsive relationship, obvious to everybody but them. While it was nice that they expressed their "love" for one another and enjoyed each other's company, the relationship overall was dark and compulsive.

Within a genuinely healthy relationship both the quality of time spent together and a deep respect and honoring for one another will be paramount. If you've got a shitty relationship you can spend every night of the week together and you can have sex seventy-five times a month and it isn't going to make a damn bit of difference. The relationship is still going to crumble or sink into self-abusive, or other-abusive, hell (or heaven depending on one's psychological mechanisms). If your relationship is one of quality and you can enjoy one another's company fully when you're together, it doesn't matter how much time you spend together, obviously within reasonable limits. If you only spent one night a week together, that one night could be perfect.

Ideally, being together never enslaves, but rather liberates. You can still be an individual and lead your own life within the context of marriage, of friendships, of community, of your job.

Otherwise, you've missed the point. If you don't allow your partner, housemates, employees or employers, and friends the space to be just who they are—you've missed the point. Relationships have to do with freedom, passion, mutual enjoyment and so on, not with the creation of an "us-against-them" unit, or with the manipulation of the other person.

Understandably, it is hard to allow that freedom to the other because when you find somebody you like you want to be with him or her, and you want to make sure that you can control this. But even manipulation for ends that seem beneficent or philanthropic is not the right foundation for an on-going, nurturing relationship.

When communion is the mood of your life you will spend private time with your mate, but contextually it won't be self-referencing and isolating. Because you are a couple you will naturally gravitate toward one another, but it won't be spending time alone in the usual, exclusive, cultic way. It will be communion. When communion is present there is no such thing as "alone." The word doesn't exist. Yet, the form will certainly appear to be of two people going off together with no one else there.

So, be with your partner or friends when they give you the go-ahead to be with them, and when they don't, you have the choice to be either miserable or happy while you're doing whatever it is you do when you're not together. If your love or friendship is not based on neurotic survival strategies, you will have no reason not to be happy.

Secret 24: How To Support and Please One Another

If you provide delight in someone's life they're alive, and their aliveness will communicate to everyone else. When somebody's happy in a relationship, they're in relationship with everything, with the universe. They're relaxed, easeful, communicative, bright, interested and wise in an organic way.

If someone has got their "head up their ass," and they don't know what their life is all about and where they are going, to support them is not to drive their head from their ass right up into their belly. To provide support is to pull their head out of their ass and help them define, with no definitions of your own, who they are and what their life is about. You draw them into communion. That's not making them over. It's allowing the Divine to become apparent.

So, to support someone is to acknowledge their true being, their essential truth and essence, and not to dwell on or belittle (or even praise) their superficial aspects, personality traits, neurotic eccentricities. Someone who is truly supported is always talented, capable, reliable, selfless and hardworking.

● ● ●

In our heart of hearts, most of us really think that what we're good at is pleasing a man or pleasing a woman—if not sexually, then socially at least.

Do you want to know how you really please a man or please a woman? *Be present for them and leave them alone.*

If someone loves you, they will open their Being to you. If someone appreciates and enjoys your company, they will radiate when they are in your presence. *Be present and leave them alone.*

How do you leave them alone? One way is to not be intrusive, manipulative, or dominating. Listen, ladies, how many men are actually going to chop their left arm off when they're slicing potatoes in the kitchen, eh? Not too many. It's true that they might nick their finger a little. But how much could it hurt for you to just let the guy use the razor-sharp knife the way *he* wants to use it, and not tell him how to do it?

And men, how many women are going to hell for sure if they act wildly happy to see one of their girlfriends, or if they act differently when they see one of their girlfriends than they act when you walk in the door? You know what I'm talking about. For example, the women are with their girlfriends, chattering away, and you're sitting there fuming: "She never treats me like that."

Why do you think she doesn't ever treat you like that? It's because you won't be present and leave her alone.

One way for men (and women) to begin to consider a kind of feminine receptivity is in this kind of dynamic. The essential feminine mood is one of support, nurturing, affection, attention. For instance, if you, man, are walking around the house and the woman is doing something and you see how it could be done better, just keep your mouth shut. Things will get done. Let her cook the way she wants. It's difficult doing that sometimes, but it is a way to begin. Don't backseat drive. Let the woman drive once in a while. Just sit in the other seat and keep your mouth shut. It's a good practical exercise to allow another person, in this case a woman if you're a man, to just do what they do in their own special way.

Secret 25: When a Love Affair is Breaking Up

Especially where relationships are concerned, don't think you're hot shit—because you aren't. Don't think you can "handle it"—because you can't. The only things you can handle are things you've handled before, and then only if you're lucky or blessed. None of us can handle anything new. The most we can do is get through a new circumstance in one piece and learn something. But "handle" them? I don't think so.

I've made a couple of big moves in my life. In the midst of them I have thrown my shoulders back and said, "I can handle it!" But it's always turned out that I didn't handle it too well at all. I could have approached the situation much differently. A couple of radical events like this convinced me that you should keep your mouth shut most of the time when you're in a state of hyper-emotionality or desperation. Verbal restraint, obviously without just repressing it all, could save a lot of pain and anxiety. It's best, most of the time, to just keep your mouth shut with your parents, with your children, with your mates and friends, because we say things, all the time, that are like grandstand gestures—desperate attempts to validate some neurotic element of our insecurities, fears, or angers. These neuroses hardly need support, and attempts to support them end up being even more depressive or dissonant to the space and circumstance.

Sometimes we act on these braggadocio claims and then we usually end up paying.

When people panic, they tend to make exaggerated and irrational gestures—grandstand plays. People tend to do that when relationships are failing. A lot of children are born in an attempt to save a relationship or a marriage, and of course that's the worse thing to do to save a floundering or unhealthy situation. To burden a child with that for the rest of its life is cruel. It's a very sad state of affairs when we're so immature that we make grandstand threats or gestures out of our inability to bring sanity to our lives.

Many people get divorced and their attitude is, "That son-of-a-bitch, I knew when I met her (or him) that she (he) was no good." If you don't take at least fifty-percent of the responsibility (and it would serve you to take more—like seventy or eighty-percent—even if it was only five-percent your fault), if you go around blaming other people and circumstances for your problems you'll never be big enough to handle anything. You won't be able to handle running out of cigarettes for a day! You won't be able to handle anything if you're always blaming your problems on everything else and not looking at your own complicity in the situation,

When, as a teenager or in my early twenties, I would leave a relationship, I would say: "I deserved better..." or, "It wasn't working out for me..." I was entirely selfish, as all of you probably have been at some times. As my affairs started to become serious, however, I learned very quickly that I was as much at fault as anyone else, and was willing to take responsibility for it (though *how* I was willing and able to is a mystery).

Grandstand plays or exaggerated gestures aren't based on patience, persistence and waiting for the right time.

Secret 26: Monogamy

I think that people should just get together monogamously and enjoy a healthy sexual relationship. Men and women should fall in love, love one another, and, just because they are insecure, not flirt with every other man or woman who comes along. Monogamy is recommended because love breeds within a field of intimacy and union.

Sex provides a kind of vulnerability that's not found elsewhere. Probably the closest thing to it might be what is shared among the survivors of a plane crash, or some other profound event in which great hardships are experienced together. You share the kind of vulnerability that there is in sex when there's real shattering, common tragedy, but in no other way. That doesn't even happen in the deepest friendships. You don't get the kind of chemical vulnerability which you do in sharing sympathy during tragedy. Your body changes when there is real chemical sympathy to other people, and most people can't share that kind of vulnerability with more than one person and not be torn apart by it internally. We're not wired that way.

In false monogamy you are limited to one person because you develop the kind of relationship that isolates the two of you against the world. The guy comes home from work and Honey says, "Did you get the raise, babe?" And he says, "No, God damn it. They promoted somebody else over me." And Honey says, "What? What! They don't treat you right at that place. You ought to look for another job. Your boss doesn't appreciate you."

They feed off one another and develop this kind of bubble to keep them apart from the world.

In true monogamy, there is no urge on the part of either person to flirt or play seductress or seductor games, or hunter games. The love of the hunt for the man is in his work, creativity, art, his passion for his wife and children. The woman nurtures her family, her man, home, environment, community, her art form. Then the world is actually one's oyster.

● ● ●

People sometimes have extraordinary experiences in new relationships where the intensity of infatuation or the desire to bond is very strong. That's why a lot of people fall for someone besides who they are currently in relationship with, but then go back right away to their original partner. They realize that extraordinary experiences were missing from their old relationships, and that they are going to be missing in the new relationship soon too.

There is something people build together over time that nothing can replace. Time can't be created in a new relationship. It may well be true that you are "old karmic mates" and you've been together over lifetimes, but you still can't rush it. You can't synthesize the element of time in relationship.

Secret 27: Avoid Conventional Relationship

You can live with a person for years without being married, but once the contract is signed, once it's made legal, powerful "programming" about what marriage is can manifest. This programming is often so deep that no matter how open or intelligent or sensitive one is, once that contract is signed it starts to mean something political, something territorial. In my experience people react to the marriage contract from strong unconscious motivations. Typically, one way of reacting is to think, "Ah, now it's mine." (Sort of the way you react to making the last payment on the car.)

A subtle strategy arises out of that type of reaction—people start taking advantage of their mates, although they really don't mean to. Maybe the husband doesn't say nice things anymore, or he doesn't tell her how good her cooking is anymore. Little things change. Once the contract is signed, once it's legal and the honeymoon is over, these considerations for one another can start to fall away very quickly.

Conventional relationship, with friends as well as with mates, usually involves ownership and territory. Whenever people are paired up, the drive to territorialize is extremely powerful; we tend to think of our friend or our mate as our property. At a party, for instance, if our mate talks with someone of the opposite sex we can get crazy. But let's face it, if your mate is seriously interested in having sex with somebody else that's too bad, really, but what are you going to do? Try to stop it? And how?

With imprisonment? With violence?

Listen. Your partner is not going to have a better relationship with you because you stopped him or her from sleeping with somebody else. You need to deal with the fact that he (or she) probably still loves you as much as ever. It's true. Sometimes people are just naive, and when they start to wake up, lots of doubts, confusions and breakdowns occur on the road to wisdom and maturity. Like in this case, maybe you were the first person your partner ever slept with. Maybe you were the "All-American Man" who wouldn't marry anyone unless she was a virgin. You made sure your wife saved herself for you. Then, it happened. One day, a few years into your marriage, your wife read *The Joy of Sex* and *Fear of Flying* and she got a tickle somewhere... Or, maybe her desire for another sexual partner is because you're a clod. After two minutes of sex you roll over and probably even say, "Thank you dear," or "Was it good for you too?" Or, you leap up and say, "How about an omelet? I'm a hell of a cook!" (Most guys are very insensitive. Most women are insensitive, too, but women can cover their insensitivity by acting warm, understanding, compassionate, dedicated, and patient. They've got a different strategy: the dedicated, hard-working, sacrifice-everything-for-her-man-and-family strategy.)

When one makes a choice to marry, that choice should not be a conventional one. The real choice is a choice to serve this other person for a lifetime. (But that is so far from our current experience in conventional society. Any organic, spiritual tradition we once had here has been obscured and smashed. We've been psychologically crippled, particularly in the Western world. Maybe we should call it DMD—Dead Man's Disease—with the emphasis on *Man*.)

Each of us should be clear about whether he or she is still rooted in propagating conventional activity in intimate life, or not. That type of propagation is a lie; it involves the "you" which is the product of society, family, environment—of everyone and everything *but* God. When one embarks on this journey of transformation one must start "right where one lives"—in one's daily activities, personal manifestations, gestures, and attitudes. Great metaphysical concepts and airy ideals are useless if one's intimate life remains isolated and crippled by habitual psychological rigidities and uninspected assumptions.

Secret 28: Defining Love

At whatever age of our lives we are at, what we think is love is mostly based on extremely inadequate experiences. If you look back, you'll see that we thought we were really mature, experienced, and worldly about love at thirty. When we're forty, we look back upon what we thought love was at thirty and say, "My God, how immature. All of the mistakes I made and the people I insulted. If only I had known." Then we're fifty and our entire perspective is more mature...fuller...richer. (The word "mature" has a lot of connotations. It doesn't just mean we're older and more experienced, but that our capacity is so much deeper and our hearts are so much fuller.) Basically, what we keep seeing is *what love isn't*, and the more we see what love isn't, the more we appreciate what it is—whatever it is.

Another thing we realize as we mature is that love is always available, and it is not dependent upon any *other*. The fourth volume of The *Alexandria Quartet*, a series of books by Lawrence Durrell, concludes that one who is in love, or one who loves when love is true, doesn't need anything outside himself or herself. In the case of the historical Mirabai, love was alive and the Beloved was present in the form of a little stone idol of Krishna. There wasn't any other consideration. And the same relationship to Love is true of many saints. The Beloved is present for many of the Christian mystics, not in the form of Jesus as much as literally in the form of some beloved icon, like a picture of Jesus or a crucifix. (Maybe in the early days there were even real artifacts around—splinters off the real cross, Virgin Mary weed, threads from Jesus' socks... or something like that.)

One comes to realize that to embody love is an outpouring, not a need or a reliance on any external taking in. Some of the most romantic and sweetly painful literary examples of love are those in which for one reason or another, the lover was denied—through death, through being taken for granted, or through simple arrogance. But the love was so full that it expressed itself anyway, despite the unconsciousness of the object of that love.

As one becomes more of a student of love, one realizes that one either loves or one studies love. There isn't anything in between. I would venture to say most of us are simply students of love, although we've probably fallen in love countless times, possibly without even knowing it.

You can't exactly define love, but what you can do is develop a question about love which will continue to be refined with more and more clarity and distinction. It is not that you are always weighing things against what love is, but your experience serves to refine the question so that your focus becomes more and more singular, less and less fuzzy. In the beginning, identification is liable to include some things in your focus that really shouldn't be there, but that all gets purified by the heat of sadhana[1].

---

1 sadhana - spiritual work or spiritual practice

Secret 29: Chemical Love, Emotional Love
and Conscious Love

In human relationships a magnetic attraction exists between both sympathetic and opposite chemistries. Opposites do attract—like the north pole and south pole of a magnet. Sympathetic chemistries attract also—we seek what mirrors us because we desire to grow, to know ourselves.

When opposites attract it can be like a jigsaw-puzzle as people try to fit into one another's matrices. And, while these relationships tend to last longer than the sympathetic attractions, because one complements the other, as long as any of our relationships are based purely on chemistry, nothing happens in terms of completeness. If two people don't share a somewhat similar aim, or perspective, the lower elements of their consciousness usually destroy whatever bonding is being established.

In chemical love, which includes basically all of our infatuations and love affairs, the laws of chemistry apply. For instance, people have a certain physical tolerance for one another that varies from individual to individual, and they just play that tolerance out. (When the tolerance is exhausted, so is the relationship.)

If we feed one another's chemistry, one another's "glands," there is only one way for us to react. It is absurd to assume that in a chemical love affair we're not going to get angry or jealous, or feel guilty, or insecure, or be free of any emotional reaction—

high, low, positive, negative, or neutral. We are bound by the limitations of our chemistry, and chemistry knows no feeling. It simply does whatever it is catalyzed to do. (And it could do anything within its nature.)

From the foundation of chemical love only, it's absurd to make promises to one another, because we're promising in our heads, not paying attention to the laws of chemistry. We promise out of belief, expectation, or projection (all from the mind), but we cannot control our chemistry and fit it into the straight-jacket of our neurotic use of language, no matter how sincere the language is in the moment of our promise.

People constantly promise fidelity, for example, but by chemical nature we're not monogamous! By spiritual nature we're absolutely monogamous, but by chemical nature we're like animals—like a cock in the barnyard who just goes around humping all the hens. The animal doesn't know what it's doing by self-reflection, of course; its activity is chemistry—pure instinct.

The same thing applies to chemical human love. It is all directed by impersonal momentum. And, as long as love remains chemical, as long as we remain sub-human, that's the kind of love affairs we always have.

With chemical love, if we're not adulterous in body, we are adulterous in mind. All of those idioms—like "variety is the spice of life," or the whole "seven-year-itch" thing, or other bullshit—are simply designed to validate chemical reactions because we are subhuman.

We don't know (and don't need to know) the totality of our own or our partner's chemistry. But we do need to develop a specific attitude of exploration, wonder, and acceptance. In studying self, therefore, we need to be aware of what is chemical, what is emotional, and what is conscious love.

● ● ●

Emotional love arises as a result of tendencies that are programmed into the psyche environmentally—by one's peer group, parents, teachers, and life circumstances. We fall in love emotionally, based on the primal strategies of survival that applied in chemical love. Starting from childhood we observe our environment and begin to develop based on these observations. In all our relationships, then, we relate strategically as a result of our chosen worldview.

Emotional love relationships tend to be extremely mercurial. Up, down, up, down, up, down. People end up actually hating one another, loving one another, and hating one another again—but not separating from one another. They can't separate because they're too dependent on each other for support. Each of their "stories" is emotionally hooked into the other. The classic co-dependent dynamic!

There are a lot of cases of emotional love around. In fact, emotional love is probably epidemic in the Western world. It is also the most difficult kind of love to transform. When you are in an "up" stage of an emotional love relationship, by God it is exhilarating, inspiring, and consuming! Therefore, it is too good to take a chance of losing by splitting up when you're in the "down" (abusive) stage. Emotional love is also the stuff of inspiration. People who are emotionally in love should always be poets or artists or knights on a quest.

You can learn about chemical love, study it, and rise beyond its domination (in the sense of knowing it well enough to not be confused by its signals), but emotional love is so totally destructive and so integral to aberrant psychological strategies that even when one gets *out* of it one rarely gets *over* it.

● ● ●

Conscious love, on the other hand, has no place for reactive and degenerative emotions. But, conscious love doesn't disregard chemistry, either—being biological creatures, we have a tendency to continue the race and are bound, to some degree, by the laws of our cellular structures and our glandular secretions.

Only conscious love can create a love affair in which the people in it are responsive to the laws of Alchemy—laws of Transformation—over and against laws of stagnation and mere maintenance. We are machines—the best in the universe, or the best in our galaxy at least, but machines nonetheless. Without conscious love there is no possibility of being different from the usual primate creatures that we are.

Conscious love touches upon more than our interpersonal human relationships. The way that human beings have developed exquisite strains of flowers is an attempt at conscious love. The breeding of the most magnificent thoroughbred horses and pure-bred dogs is another form of moving toward conscious love. In these cases we have served the optimum creation of a given species, a given channel of life, out of a desire for beauty.

Of course, these forms of conscious love have also been denigrated by the motivation for profit or power—for egoistic purposes. We didn't do it for the dog, we did it to get the prize. We didn't do it for the horse, we did it to win races and to stroke our insatiable quest for beauty. We didn't do it for the flower, but that doesn't invalidate the initial urge. We did it because that flower evoked something in us and we wanted that feeling. We sought to be gods—to create, to transform! Not knowing what conscious love is, we haven't intentionally created it but we have moved in that direction. Conscious love is the highest form of love that we can evoke.

Intuitively, the whole idea of a "super race"—the attempt to optimize this strain—is an attempt to create conscious love. But it gets subverted by our selfish, albeit subconscious, psychological motivations. We simply go about these things in the wrong fashion. We don't know what we are doing, but we are literally moved in certain directions by the demands of the Great Process of Divine Evolution[2].

When the human is communing with nature he is receiving a very primitive form of conscious love. Nature is pure. She has no psychological twists, no free ego—no worm ego, no elephant ego, no mountain or rainbow or sun ego! We can be vulnerable and freely expressive towards nature because we aren't concerned with psychic backlash. Unfortunately, we are not going to receive that from other human beings, except in very particular and conscious circumstances—such as in a working spiritual School.

Conscious love is so sacred and awesome actually, that, in a sense, the beloved falls under the spell of the lover's love and will not ever forget or leave the conscious lover. Over a period of time this love is always returned. The initial response to conscious love is to "sign on" for life, so to speak.

Being able to return that conscious love, once you're hooked, is another story, however, as is sustaining the profound heat—the tension of the transformation—that conscious love provokes. These experiential adjustments may take a lifetime to work out, but so what? What else is there to do of any value anyhow?

Conscious love does not occur by chance, but must be cultivated, engaged, activated and lived. People don't "fall" in conscious love. It comes from a tremendous amount of very hard work, one element being that you always need to observe yourself to determine whether what you want for your lover is what's best for him or her, or just your own egocentric preference.

Of course you want certain things, but what is best for the other—the object of this love? Suppose what's best for him or her doesn't involve you—for a month, for two months, for a year?

---

2 Great Process of Divine Evolution - The Will of God. It is the ongoing Process of God which includes everything seen and unseen, including life from conception to death.

Conscious love means to do whatever is best for your lover, even when it's antagonistic to what your ego would most like for yourself (itself). (Even the phrase "your lover" is ridiculous because in conscious love the whole notion of possessiveness doesn't apply. And, of course, the word "lover" has absolutely nothing to do with the common usage of the word. I only use that as a convenience to avoid a lengthy rhetorical articulation each time.) The person trying to develop conscious love is always involved in these crises, every single day—over work, over what time to get up in the morning, about how often to have sex and what kind of sex to have, regarding what to eat or how many vitamins to take, about when to have children, how many to have, and how to bring them up, over how to treat in-laws, when to see parents...and on and on...every single day... over and over and over. But, these crises only occur at the level of mind—psychologically or mentally based—not in the body.

"What is the best for my lover?" Whatever it is, that is what you need to surrender to. (And that only comes through submission to Divine Influence. The ego itself can never make these choices. Only the Will of God is intelligent enough to have the necessary perspective.)

Sometimes what is best for your lover is very painful for him or her. Sometimes your lover has to accomplish something at the price of sweating blood, and they will resist that right down to the wire. If you have the power to enable your lover to accomplish what he or she needs to accomplish for themselves, you need to engage that, even if it means a tremendous amount of stress on your part, and even if they are going to fight it all the way.

You cannot be a conscious lover in the sense I am describing here without God being at the heart of your relationship with whomever you couple. When you are a conscious lover with your partner, you are perfectly attuned to the spiritual dimensions of the Intelligence of God. If you try to make these decisions out of learned data or trained experience, at best you'll be functioning from an educated guess. Certainty is a matter of God's Will making decisions through human instinct, never from a mental construct or compilation of knowledge.

When you consciously love you can sense the perfection in your lover, not as a human but as an element of the creation of God. No matter what the "shell" looks like, no matter how many good or bad habits the other has, no matter how crazy, you can always sense that perfection, that essence. And, at the cost of everything in your life, even at the cost of sanity, you want to evoke that perfection in your lover. That's conscious love. That type of ideal relationship has to be cultivated. That has to be worked, trained. You didn't grow up being able to do that in this society. The greatest accomplishment we could ever hope for is to become a conscious lover.

Most of us are not even consciously tolerant. (There is a huge difference between simply being tolerant and being consciously tolerant.) People are a mass of tendencies, habits, and neuroses. Conscious tolerance is the recognition of those tendencies and the understanding that you're going to have to relate to other people with all of their habits and neuroses, not wait until they no longer animate what "rubs you wrong." If you wait for that you will wait forever...maybe longer. Maybe in five years they will be a little bit different, or maybe they will never be different, but either way that is who they are!

If you can see that spark of perfection in your lover, you have to keep relating both with that as well as with their surface textures, until they are being different, until they do act in alignment with their innate perfection. That's conscious tolerance.

The tolerance that most of us experience, however, is not a tolerance by choice. It's a tolerance almost of necessity. We are tolerant because we have to be, because we just want to get along with one another, because we don't care, or because we don't want to create hassles and problems. We are tolerant for our own survival, not consciously tolerant for our beloved. We don't see the perfection in one another. Instead, we are always bitching and moaning, and when other peoples' faults get to us, if we have enough control of will we bite our lips. We are tolerant! We don't want to create waves, so we are tolerant.

But both humility and conscious tolerance are required for the conscious lover. The conscious lover could be a hundred times closer to his or her own perfection than their beloved is, but humility is always required. If you live for the beloved, what's the difference how perfect you are? You don't go around lording your perfection over others.

Over time, people who submit themselves to the alchemy of conscious love return that love in kind, become capable of it out of their own strength and process. There is a perfect giving, and a perfect taking in the reciprocity of Adoration and Devotion. There is always giving and taking. There is never a disagreement as to who gives when and who takes when. There is a giving, and a relaxing into that giving; and there's a taking, and relaxing into that taking on both or all peoples' parts. Obviously, this applies between a man and woman, between friends of the same gender, and between human and God as well (in fact it better!).

We must know what we are doing. In the creation of conscious love we are working with a chemical factory that is more sensitive technologically than any chemical factory in the world. If we do not have *Knowledge,* that is, *if we are not willing to know the relationship of the functional and formal world to the movement of God, if we are not willing to understand the hierarchy of the chemistry and energies that meet and interplay and form this body,* we will kill one another. We'll make our mates sick, miserable, insane. Literally, we will destroy one another over a lifetime. It is not simply that we will create some type of psychosomatic illness. People will actually destroy one another if Knowledge is not present.

Love is not enough; there must be Knowledge. If we simply love but don't fulfill the Law[3] we die. The conscious lover doesn't mind giving up whatever is necessary for the beloved; and ideally the beloved has Knowledge as well, so they can feed one another and free one another.

---

3   The Law - The sacrificial nature of all elements of existence, which can be consciously lived. "Everything is food for everything else."

Secret 30: No Self Equals Love. Self Equals No Love.

You can't have love and be separate from God. "Well, I'm going to maintain my separation from God because, after all, I've got dreams and aspirations and things I have to do with my life. I need to be free and I need to be creative and I need to dance and sing and sew and make children and take care of my man, first. I'll have time for God when I've done all I need to do in my life. Then I'll be loving..."

No you won't! Maybe you'll be conventionally a little more gentle and appropriate than most people; but love is something that cannot exist separate from God. As long as your "I" is functioning, as long as it's "you" who wants love, and "you" who is giving love, it's not love. It may be affection, it may be caring, it may be concern, consideration, understanding, sympathy, empathy—but love, no! Not love. No matter how exalted you feel when your lover gives you a rose, it isn't love. It's exaltation, not love. It is all bullshit—like how your heart melts or your eyes mist as you gaze at your mate or your child! Love cannot be present when you are separate from God. It can't be.

It is very fashionable these days to approach love as if it were a commodity. We all mistakenly think that ego is going to keep its autonomy, and we're going to get love as the final gift for being "good." No way! There are some fundamentalist Christians who are so good that if people got medals for being good they would not be able to walk, they would be so weighted down from the medals on their chests. You don't get love by being good. You get love by disappearing, by dissolving. As long as *you* exist, love won't. When *you* cease to exist, *love* will—immediately. Just like that.

Perfect combination: no self equals love, self equals no love. There are no degrees. The first thing you have to do is give up all your little "i's," because you aren't even going to get to know who your "I" is as long as you've got a world war going on inside your psyche. First you have to bring all your little "i's" to a kind of center, so that your three centers (the intellect, the heart, and the moving center) are essentially sympathetic and not functioning at cross-purposes. Recommended conditions of meditation, exercise, and study do that. Then, once you get to feel like you're "hot shit" because you do those things and are in a pretty high state most of the time, and you're detached, and you've got revelation upon vision upon satori[4] coming through, then you've got to give all that up too. Finally you've got to go through the world naked, free of an "I" that defends you and protects you and makes sure you're always right (even when you're more wrong than wrong). So that's the story.

As long as you maintain the attempt to dramatize and glorify your "I," you will never realize God. You have no choice, no prayer, not a quarter of a percent, not even a tenth of a percent chance. If you begin to be willing to give that up, the Work will proceed quickly. You'll fly through it. The crucifixion will be hard, but over soon.

Some of you have been hanging on the cross whining and complaining for years and it's your own damn fault. There is nobody to blame but yourself with your perverse, stubborn refusal to surrender your "I." It's not, "But I can't." You're stubborn, stubborn, stubborn. So there you have it. Nothing to it. Life is so simple.

---

4   satori - sudden enlightenment, in Zen teaching.

Really, there are only two things—the "I" and the transcendence of "I." Instead, we make this infinite range of considerations. "What about this, what about that, what about...life after death?... When does the soul enter the body?...Is abortion moral? ...What about men, women, life, death, infinity?... and how long will General Hospital be on TV?"

Maybe we all ought to enter the TV world; it's a nice life there. We'd all be preserved just the way we are and never grow old. We are a culture of idiots, and this is an intellectual wasteland; an entire country can be polarized over whether some TV character is going to be assassinated or not! If it wasn't so sad, it would be the most incredible, bizarre joke known to man. Well, there you have it once again, hmm?

Secret 31 : Building Love and The Sacred Marriage

In the book *Chasm of Fire* by Irina Tweedie, her Sufi Teacher said, "Love is produced." Love doesn't just happen. You have to create and maintain it, and repair it when that is necessary. The same is true of relationship. If the heat fades a bit, you've got to recreate it. You can't bring it back from the past because the past is dead. To enter a marriage you should recognize that the commitment must include the mutual creation of its continued existence.

Within marriage the content of communion tends to ebb and flow, and so there will always be hot points and cool points, as in any relationship. If you commit yourself to a marriage, then, you shouldn't expect that things will always be hot and juicy every minute. When you hit a cool point you shouldn't think to yourself, "Hey, things used to be great between us, let's get it back the way it was." Instead, think, "Here we are now. What are we going to do now?"

Men and women both sometimes go through the "seven-year itch," or the "fourteen-year itch." Some men experience wanderlust from about age forty through age sixty. Women often have a deep dissatisfaction with men's failure to serve "Woman" in them. All of this gets compounded by the contemporary culture's love affair with self-centered irresponsibility and narcissism, and thus makes long-term relationship a tremendous challenge.

Still, despite the many problems and obstacles, I'm strongly

110

in favor of long-term, committed relationships. People who live together in intimate circumstances for long periods of time (and anything over seven years is getting to be a really long period of time these days), will develop something potentially valuable with one another that they wouldn't develop under any other circumstances. They develop a matrix which, if it is recognized and used, can be profoundly transformational.

We need to be capable of devoting ourselves to this building of love. After all, we're not going to be able to float for a lifetime on the initial "buzz"—that first wave of infatuation, even if it was somewhat beyond the usual fleshy attraction (as in, "At last I've found my soul-mate"). I have found that the more ethereal or astral aspects of relationship will take care of themselves if the other aspects, the ordinary, commonsense responsibilities such as care, honesty, willingness to lose face, and a sense of humor (especially about oneself), are handled with impeccable integrity.

Marriage is not just a cultural habit or law. Nor is it the empty ritual and overblown drama of the contemporary scene. The elements and expectations of marriage in conventional society are hardly indicative of the actual sanctity of Real marriage. And "Real" marriage doesn't need to be validated by a religious ceremony or governmental authorization.

Marriage means an agreement to be intimate, not only sexually, but intimate in friendship at levels of soul, at levels of deep organic being. Marriage is an agreement to serve one another for a lifetime, to be honest and open (to who one's partner is as well as who he or she thinks they are, or who he or she is afraid of being), and to be communicative and loving and compassionate in the face of it all. Obviously, in a "successful" marital relationship, both people have a similar disposition of acceptance and adoration. (But, that's quite unusual to have both people in the same place at the same time, or even in the same place at all.) Attitude is the key, however. One person can be terribly jealous and be greatly disturbed for a while, but as long as both partners are willing to deal with it and love each other anyway, the couple will get through it. What's important is the attitude—allowing your mate freedom, as well as recognizing her (or his) service to you. It works in both ways.

Marriage implies a choice to give the other the freedom to be a little insensitive once in a while, and even take you for granted. Serving means a choice to not extract vengeance when your partner gets a little moody, even though you know exactly how to hurt him (or her) back. (Once you've spent a couple of months with someone you know where the vulnerable points are. Isn't it odd that one of the first things we do with our intimates is collect data on what gives them pain emotionally?)

Marriage also implies permission for the other to grow, to have the freedom to respond in whatever way is necessary where essential *being* is concerned, and to develop a deep and ultimately meaningful relationship to God.

Serve one another in marriage—but not in the fundamentalist sense in which the man dominates, controls, and abuses the woman. The Patriarchy is not enlightened. (I don't know if it ever has been.) The Patriarchy's marriage laws are inherently biased and unjust. So, distinctions need to be made between marriage, the assumption, and marriage as an Objective type of relationship. This latter type of marriage exists in the eyes of God and means being responsive, as individuals, to God first, and then responsive as individuals to both the situation and to one's partner. This objective type of relationship is a view from a larger perspective—one which considers that the couple is literally affecting the world. Consequently, we must beware of getting so wrapped up within our own little closed bubble that we forget we actually are "the world" itself.

Real Marriage is an elegant formalization of two people's commitments to work together in a way that reflects their relationship to the Divine. Essentially, it's a kind of formal bond entered into in the spirit of *sadhana,* or spiritual practice, not in any spirit of morality. This is also the archetypal expression of marriage. When one becomes a real student of God, of course, all of these elements—of responsiveness to God, situation, mate—exist simultaneously. There is no hierarchy. One is not placed before the other. Such a student's overall response is natural and spontaneous, so whatever needs to arise, arises in the way it needs to for the Divine Process.

Marriage at the level of soul or spirit (the upperworld considerations, in the shamanistic worldview), the details of everyday life (the middleworld aspects), and the dark secrets of the underworld of each individual—these are all included and all get worked out in this process of "building love," since such a process is actually one of alchemical transformation.

The formal rite of marriage should be indicative of having reached a level of maturity in the Work (spiritual work) in which you can free your partner with unconditional support to do his or her *sadhana.* But, don't misunderstand this definition. If you even mention this alchemical or objective concept to most people they will say, "Oh, you mean like an open marriage?" People commonly think of "freeing one's partner" only in sexual terms.

Sacred marriage means to create an overall environment of sanctuary for one another's spiritual work or practice. You free your partner to do the spiritual work he or she needs to do, while you also provide your absolute support. And all this is done within the context of intimacy, tenderness, and sexual communion. Sacred marriage frees the partners, rather than controls them. Marriage, in a sense, is vowing that you will never complicate your mate's *sadhana* with envy, pettiness, competition, or greed.

To build love—with mates, children, friends—is worth whatever price you have to pay, even if the price is peace of mind and physical health. To build love provides some quality of

Being that does not stop, or cease, when the body-mind-complex dies. And, to build Love produces "muscles" that are useful, and even crucial, in many other areas of *sadhana*.

Building Love will demand sacrifice and create heat, because every self-dramatizing and Divine-refusing bone in one's body (both physic and physical) will attempt to undermine and confuse the clarity and momentum one is developing in building and maintaining Love. This process demands qualities that are extraordinary. But the result is also extraordinary in that it raises one from the gutter of Ego to the position of a Devotee of God.

Secret 32: Love Never Ends

People are going to phase through some radical behavioral changes in the course of their relationships. You must be prepared for that with your mates and your friends, and be willing to recognize that a phase, as difficult as it may be, is just a phase. It is temporary, even though some of them last for an extended period of time. Love does not depend on behavioral changes. It can't. It is not Love if it does, obviously. But, what we commonly call love *is* affected by behavioral changes. "You're not the same person I married," someone may say in alarm.

You wouldn't want anybody to be the same person you married or you would have married a log or a stone! But, sometimes, especially when you move into the sphere of Divine Influence, the behavioral changes can be pretty radical. If Love is present, however, the Love is not affected by the behavioral changes even if some adjustments are necessary. These changes in the other person may annoy you, but Love will not be at issue. (Sometimes, for instance, your ability to be at ease with somebody in the same room may be at issue for a temporary period, but Love should never be threatened or weakened by transformational changes.)

Once love enters your life, if it is Love, it's permanent. It remains regardless of whether you continue in a personal relationship or not.

Real Love involves risk and terror. Everything on which you consciously base your presence in the world has to go in the

---

115

face of real Love. "What if I don't come back?" you ask. Well, that's the risk!

We don't know what kind of risk there might be in love because we never know what form Love might take. When you first thought of love, you probably thought about a benign life with someone—a nice family, travelling once in a while, good food and stylish clothes. Maybe you took a few risks and married somebody your family didn't approve of. But, when you really get into love, you never know what form it might take.

Maintaining relationship puts you at emotional risk, but only in the psychological domain. Love itself is not at issue, because Love is constant. Stay with Love. There are problems, of course, but to put yourself at emotional risk is to stay in the relationship, to work out the problems. To avoid all risk is to go somewhere else when the heat is on, or to keep things light, airy, and humorous, so as not to deal with the heat. To avoid risk is to always pull yourself out of the heat.

Love and relationship are unconnected. It's very rare that two people in a relationship both have Love, even if they can say "I love you" a million times. But, such a relationship is still worth any risk. Take the risk! If you Love and the other person doesn't, then maybe they will at some point, or maybe they won't; but Love and relationship are disconnected. They are not in the same domain.

If two people have Love, and their reference for that is one another, what they have to realize is that: 1. they have Love, and 2. they happen to be together. It's not that they love because of one another, but rather that Love is present in spite of a personal relationship. How fine! They have Love, for one reason or another—it doesn't matter why. They have Love, and it expresses itself in the relationship.

Love is like God. It's both grounding and exhilarating. You never lose it. It is always there. You don't fade in and out of genuine Love. Terror, envy, greed, passion, or any kind of emotion may arise, but you never lose Love. To say, "I'm out of Love, because something went wrong with the relationship," is not to have ever had Love. If you have had Love, you will *always* Love, whatever the circumstance.

• • •

People commonly think they want a relationship, but there is no such thing as "a relationship." There is only *relationship*. There is no *relationship* when you have "a relationship."

This is an esoteric, dharmic consideration of language. But it is also true. It's also a contradiction in terms: "A relationship" denies what *relationship* is.

• • •

If you are loving someone, and your attention is on that one, you are using God as a bridge; but if you love someone and *Love* itself is the focus, not who you love, then you are going directly to the Source. When you take the direct approach, who you love gets to be loved objectively, but doesn't get to be stroked in the neurotic way. The ultimate form of relationship is that kind in which two people maintain a successful working bond or communion that is full of affection, compassion, honesty and intimacy, because both of them have their attention on *Love,* and not on one another. Then, because you are surrendered to the Will of God through the great Process of Divine Evolution, relationship is what spontaneously shows up for you. This is different than being in "a relationship" based on loneliness or expectations.

The communion that people in a real Community feel with one another is not because they begin looking for that. It's because everybody's primary focus is their work. Out of that arises camaraderie. The more radically our focus is on the Work, the more dramatically camaraderie arises.

Secret 33: Using Elements of Human Love
to Consider Love of the Beloved[5]

"You must be especially careful not to breathe upon a loved
human the Divine communion that more properly belongs to
the Beloved, although you can mirror that Beloved to the other.
If you make the mistake of investing in human beings the love
that belongs to the Beloved, you run the risk of blowing them
out by the intensity of feeling you project. Almost inevitably,
they must escape and you are left with an immensity of loss
and bereavement." (Jean Houston, *The Search for the Beloved*,
Los Angeles: Celestial Arts, 1988.)

You can be in deep, caring, affectionate, impeccable loving
relationship with spouse, children, parents, friends, but there
is a different quality of love one has for the Beloved than for
any human being—even for one's "soul-mate," assuming there
is such a thing. It's very popular these days to parrot the new
age teaching that you need to worship your mate as the god or
goddess that he or she truly is. That's a very dangerous teaching.

On the basic human level, we can be touched by the wonder
of life, and that can open our heart. That can happen through
the love of another, or through loving another, or through a

---

5 Beloved - in the Sufi tradition, the Divine as an object of love (who may or may
not be personified), as regarded by one who has been submitted to the Will of
God. Also called the Guest, or the Friend. In Baul terms, the Beloved is *Maner
Manush* — "the Man of the Heart." When not capitalized in this book, "beloved"
refers to an object of human love.

catalyst that isn't human. The relationship between two is analogous to the relationship between lover and Beloved. "As above, so below." So, in our yearning to find the Beloved, we can meet another human being who represents that for us, through some kind of twist of circumstance and perception. If we allow ourselves to be touched by the representation, and if we are able to make distinctions, we can be very much in love with the person, and not fall into the trap that Jean Houston describes. The mistake would be in thinking, "I've found the Beloved,"— over and against, "my beloved."

Some human love can form a trinity with the Beloved. In other words, if two people have a common love for the Beloved, that can be an element in their love for one another and can make for an extremely potent relationship.

The archetypal forms of Krishna and Radha, Parvati and Shiva, and Ram and Sita are images of the Lover having found the Beloved. They shouldn't conjure the image of the perfection of "human" love. When we superimpose our image of human love on these images, we may have nice role models, but we're essentially using Benediction incorrectly. Besides, at some point in all of those cases the Beloved has gone away, or there has been some form of separation between Lover and the Beloved. You need to understand that it's the separation that enables the Beloved to be found, through longing. Every manifestation of Shiva leaves his consort for a time and says, "I might not be back. I have to go do penance for 15,000 years or something. Wait here."

One uses the elements of the human relationship to consider loving the Beloved, making the proper distinction. The proper distinction is made by realizing that as much as you may love a person, they are not the Beloved. Shams-i-Tabriz was the representation of the Beloved for Rumi, and Layla was that for Majnun. Rumi could have used the name "Shams" and the personage of that man as his tangent point to the Beloved. In

119

fact, in his poetry there are indications that Shams is just a name. In the extended version of the story of Layla and Majnun, Majnun eventually wins Layla, and she agrees to marry him, but by the time they are to get married, he's gone. Once he actually realizes Layla the woman, he's gone. He doesn't consummate the marriage. He doesn't want anything to do with her. She's sitting there on the bed, and he wanders out of the tent, saying, "Layla, Layla..."

So, you can use the elements of human love—like tenderness, compassion, exaltation and surrender—to consider Love of the Beloved. Relationship is the first thing you work on, and then once the relationship is going, you work with the question of going deeper and deeper into Love.

Secret 34: Once in Love You Must Pursue It To the End

It's important not to function the same way in relationships that arise within the context of a life dedicated to God as in ordinary relationships. The end result of Real Love is absorption in the object of that Love to the degree that there is no self reference. Until that point, the self-reference that remains creates yearning, distress, and sometimes emotional pain, and there is nothing to do about that, except love more.

When people fall in love in the usual way, they say, "Why should I love more? It just means more pain. Before I was in love I didn't feel any of this." But the point is you can't love less and you can't stay stationary, so even though it looks like to love more means more pain, the only way out is through. So you must keep throwing yourself more into love until you are consumed by it. There are no other answers; there is no easy way out. Once Love has captured you, you must allow it to consume you or there will be pain, distress, yearning, separation. There is no in-between. Once captured, captured. Once bitten, bitten. You can't get out of it, so if you haven't "fallen" into love yet, now is the time to consider what it means. There are no half-way measures. Once Love has touched you, you must pursue it to the end.

When you fall in love, there's always some degree, some remnant of the conventional desire to have it the way you've learned you should have it—to possess the object of love, to have the other person wait on you hand and foot, speak the way you like, look the way you like, treat you with sensitivity, romance and delicacy. That's a normal and understandable desire. However, with this Love of a different order, the only way to deal with the yearning, the desire, and the pain of separation from the object of love, is to be consumed by the Love itself. There is no in-between state. Until you are consumed, there is pain, desire, unfulfilled longing, but once consumed, consumed forever. Once Love has captured you even a tiny little bit, there is no way out but through.

So if you haven't fallen in love yet, there is still the chance to run as far away from this as you can. Don't pursue spiritual life, don't think of God, don't wonder. If you haven't been bitten yet, and you don't want to be, get out quickly...run away fast. Don't have anything to do with this business until another lifetime, when you're ready. Because once you're trapped, the only way out is through—by being consumed by Love.

When you're consumed by Love, there is no self-reference. There's no "one" to be hurt, distressed, or in pain and desire. There is no individual to reference against these things, because *your* desire *is* the desire of the Lover. If the Lover's desire is not to be with you, then that's your desire too. No pain, no anguish, no misery...just, "Well, those are the cards I have been dealt." Of course, a Lover does have to sacrifice. But, once you are consumed in that Love, then the word sacrifice doesn't even apply anymore.

It's my job to get you through to the other side. Actually, it's really not my job to get you through, because I can't. It's my job to "herd" you properly, so at least you don't get lost in the mountains, so at least you don't fall in the creek and drown. That much I can do, if you give me the chance.

PART IV

The Cultures, Polarities and Essential Energies of Men and Women

Central to Lee Lozowick's vision is the creation of community supported by a God-centered culture—one which provides a viable alternative to the dehumanizing elements of the culture at large. In his terms, culture is something that encompasses a complete education from conception through death (including what it means, essentially, to be a man or a woman), thus setting the whole context for how one lives one's life.

In this section he points in the direction of enlivened male culture and enlivened female culture, expressing the uniqueness and the power of each. With that foundation he explores the essential nature of the masculine and the feminine polarities, leading to the focal consideration of Becoming Woman.

Secret 35: The Nourishment of Men's and Women's Cultures

When I was young, all my parents' friends and their wives or husbands would come to parties at our house. Most of the men and many of their wives were artists. They were friends not just by acquaintance but by ideal and feeling, by purpose, by aim. The atmosphere of these parties was one of tremendous communion—warm and full.(I could never appreciate this as a child, but when I got to be thirty-years-old, boy, did I wish I could be at those parties again. Just to sit there and soak up that atmosphere!)

Everybody would get together and socialize, and then we'd move into the dining room for dinner. The couples would generally sit together, although sometimes they wouldn't...it was very loose. After dinner, the men would always go to the living room and the women would always go into the kitchen. (Although every once in a while one of the women would go into the living room to talk with the men.)

If anything felt better than people coming to dinner, it was those after-dinner conversations. They had a different flavor, a different intensity than the dinner conversations with all the couples together, but the richness was overwhelming. It was amazing to walk into the living room where the men were discussing art or politics or whatever they were discussing (it made no difference), and to feel the depth of communion there. I had no reference for what it was exactly, and I didn't feel a part of it (and neither did I feel excluded at all, just curious but uninterested none-the-less). But the feeling was, and still is, unmistakable and unforgettable.

The women (many of whom were successful, well-known artists in their own right, with their work in museums and their own gallery exhibitions) went into the kitchen. They would do the dishes and talk together there.

For ages, the dynamics of a men's culture and a women's culture expressed in traditional tribal situations, and even in larger but still traditional social environments, have worked brilliantly. Remembering my own experience, they worked even thirty years ago. When the couples sat together at the dinner table, talking with each other, there was a relaxed, loose and wonderful atmosphere, with everyone in communion. When the men went into the living room and women went into the kitchen, there was no break in the communion. Those women who went into the kitchen weren't repressed. They weren't frustrated at not being in the living room with the men. They didn't sit in the kitchen and talk about passing the ERA (Equal Rights Amendment), and how when ERA passed they were going to march into the living room and be a part of the men's conversation. The men talked about what inspired and excited them and the women talked about what excited and inspired them, and it was often the same thing, but there was something about the distinction of cultures that was extremely beneficial, proper, and fulfilling. The women in communion in the kitchen and the men in communion in the living room were each more in communion with the other group than they would have been if everyone had been in one physical space together.

Look at what goes on today in mixed parties. What goes on is not communion. The room is full of tension, great pretenses towards happiness and satisfaction, and posturing for position and seduction. Everyone's focus is on who's looking at who...who's going to sleep with who tomorrow night or next week...who's wearing what. The level of sexual tension is unbelievable, and not quite unbearable but certainly "tacky" to anyone with a touch of elegance and sophistication. That's what goes on today because men aren't with other men and women aren't with other women. The weak, insecure, confused psyche says there's something wrong with that.

There's nothing wrong with that! It's a wonderful, amazing phenomenon.

My father would come out of those evenings with the men glowing! He loved being with his male friends. He loved sitting at dinner being with everybody, and he loved the family. But he loved being with his men friends because those gatherings were different than family gatherings. With the men he was "fed" a different meal—not better, but definitively different.

When you look at someone you love and they are freely and spontaneously happy, that feeds the relationship of the couple. When you see the person you are in relationship with being really in communion with another person of the same sex, your relationship is served inestimably. You may have fought for two weeks. You can be at the point of killing one another, but when you see the person you've been fighting with, "tooth and nail" for two weeks, and he or she is experiencing a "free moment[1]," right away you love him or her again. That recognition inflames the heat of communion—your essential heart communion.

Most of us have reference points for the use of men's culture and women's culture. Clearly defined men's and women's cultures provide a crucial, even necessary element in relationships.

The nature of a men's culture and a women's culture is not to isolate energies and thus make a clear distinction between the masculine and the feminine. (To make those cultures some-

---

1 free moment - the mood of enlightenment; a moment characterized by freedom from the usual separative consciousness.

what exclusive is only a stage that we pass through.) Those differences should be evident in any case. Rather, the nature of men's and women's culture is a matter of nutrition. There is an exclusive type of "food" that men produce for men and that women produce for women, and there's no substitute for that. There is no prejudice or bias involved. It is a simple, objective fact.

Men often seem to find it easier to look for this certain nutrient from women. To get that from men, then, they will have to engage the same form of relationship towards men that they have with women—without the sexual part. To ideally be in a relationship to a mate, one must be able to relate to him or her the same way one relates to members of the same sex when in communion with them. That sheds additional light on the need for a men's culture and women's culture. Almost all of us have had the experience of communion with someone of the same sex. When we have some sensing for that feeling of communion, we can begin to appreciate a men's culture and a women's culture, what that means and how that can feed us. The separate cultures are generally free of men-women games, especially when it is a true culture of intimacy and bonding, not just a group hanging out together. When you realize the freedom of a relationship to someone of the same sex, and you can apply that essence to a relationship with a mate, you've got it. There are a lot of other details, but that's the significant foundation.

Secret 36: Universal Polarities

Man is creator, woman is created. Man, however, cannot exist outside of creation. So the myth of Adam and Eve, in which woman is created out of man is actually backwards. God created Woman first, and out of Woman came man. If you're a man who is trying to be a macho hero, realizing that man came out of woman can be very sobering! In all actuality, man owes everything to woman. Until man begins to honor woman for who she truly is, for what each individual woman represents in relationship to the feminine polarity of all reality, the ultimate consideration of men and women in personal relationship is practically impossible.

The universe is a dynamic entity, not a static entity, and its dynamism comes from the eternal play of these polarities. Within every element of creation that polarity is both symbolically and actually manifested. Man and woman—the physical masculine and feminine genders—are symbolic of the polarity of the universe. (Now, the so-called Christians call the polarities "God" and "the Devil." For them, "God" is obviously the male polarity and "the Devil" is the female polarity, which is why many Christians are emotionally and psychically crippled, not to mention shamelessly patriarchal. The unconscious women-hatred in many so-called "organized religions" is too obvious to even comment on.)

Many therapeutic models assume that we need to synthesize the male and female aspects of ourselves into a consistent whole. But, that's not my understanding. I think that the male and female aspects of consciousness, or being, are absolutely distinct, and I've come to the conclusion that synthesizing male and female is essentially impossible. One needs to recognize what each of these polarities is, clearly, and that recognition will give one the ability to work with the polarities without conflict and to build a being that is bigger than both of them, or either of them separately. (This being doesn't subsume the uniqueness of each polarity, but uses them in its own larger process. Something else *does* get created, but that something else is created because the other two forces, male and female, provide "food" for possibility, for creation—not because parts of those two forces combine to make a third force.) Essentially, the synthesis is in working with each of the polarities fully, not with a literal integration.

An established premise here is that creation is evolutionary, and creation is going to evolve no matter what we do. We can participate in creation consciously, by serving it, or just be carried along on its wave. In other words, our role in that can be supportive or not. On the one hand, our awareness of male and female polarities is not crucial to the evolutionary process, since our ability to be essentially that which we have been created as has nothing to do with the ultimate Divine process. (That is bigger than us and won't wait for us.) On the other hand, however, if we ever want to align ourselves with this process, that is, to be conscious, then an understanding of that dynamic of male/female is crucial. Polarity is an aspect of essentially everything, including our being and consciousness. And God is polar in all of creation whether we acknowledge it or not.

Recognizing that this polarity exists, both within us and on a larger scale, should be obvious. At one level, this polarity is integral to our whole psychological makeup: it explains why we're shy, aggressive, angry, or insecure. On another level, even the path to transcendence is going to be through the dynamic of polarities.

The masculine aspect of existence has to do with the texture or matrix from which all arises (Shiva), and the feminine aspect has to do with form (Shakti). Man is consciousness, woman is manifestation. Consciousness is the underlying texture without substance; it is not a "thing" but is the ground within which things arise. Form and manifestation are things; they have Being.

Each polarity has its own very specific characteristics. It's tremendously helpful in working with both the persona and with transcendence, therefore, to be able to characterize what's masculine and what's feminine.

You begin to make these distinctions with study—just plain book-learning—and with plain, open-eyed observation of yourself and the world around you. Then you follow up with what Gurdjieff meant when he used the term "self-observation." If you observe yourself—what feels aligned to you as a man (or as woman), and what feels characteristically different, even though it's a part of your being—then, with some practice, you'll be able to define what is instinctually masculine and what is instinctually feminine.

Usually, the peak of this instinctual knowing of masculinity and femininity happens (or should) at puberty. But, in our culture, we rarely have the experience or the expertise to articulate these distinctions, so they often sink into the unconscious and are not a resource we can usually tap or use. For an adult woman, maybe the closest thing to that instinct surfacing would occur during menstruation. This is why in some Tantric methods, the most optimum time to have sexual relations is when a woman is having her period. Of course, in many new-age communities, that's the time you're told to avoid sex. In fact, in many traditions women are totally isolated during menstruation. What a loss! This avoidance and isolation, it seems to me, has to do with the blanket repression, in our culture, of both the feminine aspect as well as the repression of the right-brain functions.

Essentially, if we allow "surrender to the Will of God" to be our force of animation, we shall find a perfect balance between male and female chemistry. If ego is the force of animation, however, sooner or later we're going to have a lot of problems. If our structure doesn't have the necessary fluidity, if we can't move between the two polarities as needed, how can we possibly relate to the Divine?

Psychotherapy can soften us; it can take down fences. We need to be as masculine and as feminine as necessary and have a reciprocal flow of those energies without any handicaps. As we are able to do that, sometimes we'll be very feminine, sometimes we'll be very masculine, sometimes we'll be almost androgynous—but ego won't be making the decision about what manifestation is needed in a given situation. When ego makes the decision, it's always strategic for ego's purposes, never for God's needs.

For a man and a woman to manifest the symbolic polarities of the universe in relationship to each other, all personal issues have to be resolved, or at least seen as irrelevant. Personal issues include sexual issues, possession issues, and space issues, like, "This is my favorite chair. I don't want you sitting in it." In other words, all the elements involved in the first three chakras need to be no-problematical—free of neurotic demands and aberrated manifestations.

So we have an interesting situation in contemporary society. We have an entire culture of women and an entire culture of men, in which men do not express or enliven the appropriate texture or matrix. In fact we, as a culture, literally have no reference for this type of knowledge since it has been absent from our educational facilities for so long. We don't even know that there are options to our dead, conditioned viewpoint. And women, not having the appropriate matrix to relate to, do not express themselves as the essential Feminine. They have no true polar opposite to magnetize to. The polar opposite they are given to reflect is a patriarchal, misogynous, psychologically-aberrated, ignorant one. No wonder we are all so frustrated and empty. Manifestation does not express the true nature of Woman because there's no essential Masculine in the world to relate to. We have a culture of women with no ground in which they can become *Women* because men have denied this primal ground for a foundation of weakness, anger and fear.

Occasionally, a woman becomes Woman anyway, by accident, because women are essentially feminine anyway, but there's no western culture in which such possibilities are suggested or appreciated let alone recognized when they occur.

A culture that has really impressed me is the women's culture in India. It's becoming less and less impressive because the country is becoming more "modern," competitive and greedy, but still there is a clearly defined women's culture there.

Women in India have historically been considered to be property, and at five or six-years-old are engaged to be married, with the choice of mate arranged by her parents. (It's still very common in rural India although less so in the big cities.) Indian women have many limitations to their freedom of possibilities (again except to some degree in the cities).

In America, a woman can be a telephone repair-person, or drive a taxi. In India, if a woman drove a taxi, she'd probably be shot. It's just not done. As a result, the women's culture in India has been forced to evolve and develop into one that is incredibly rich and potent, and very self-contained, in order for women to fulfill themselves and not feel completely impotent and beaten up by the men. And, what has impressed me the most has been the brightness—the physical, auric brightness—

of the rural women. There is tremendous power in that. There isn't any cowering in the women because the men treat them like property. In the West there is still so much inter-gender pettiness and competition. I have never seen anything in America or in Europe like the strength within the Indian culture. There is a little more of that strength in some of the European countries, but it's absolutely barren and non-existent in America.

Secret 37: Becoming Men

Twenty or thirty years ago men were real "macho." They had no feeling and no sensitivity for what and who women were, and of course women reacted to that (at last!), and the whole feminist movement arose as a result. Now men are trying to get in touch with their feminine sides and are working to become soft, considerate, gentle, and so on. But, in a recent magazine article, Robert Bly, the poet, said that all of these "ideal men" have no energy.

Bly said that everywhere he goes he talks to couples. He has observed that the male partners generally look like they should be ideal mates: they're soft, responsive to women, tender, in touch with their feminine energy, and they honor a woman's point of view, individuality and femininity. But, they have no energy. They have no juice. And Bly said, something is *very wrong*.

Bly has written a book called *Iron John* (New York: Vintage Press, 1990) on the significance and archetypal communication of fairy tales and myths. One of these tales is called "The Iron Man," a traditional myth that was originally recorded by the Grimm Brothers. It goes something like this:

Hunters in the village keep disappearing. More men are sent to look for those who have disappeared, and they disappear too. Then, this hunter, who is out of work, comes to town. He goes around asking if anyone has work for him to do, but the people keep telling him about all these other hunters who have disappeared. So, he goes out with his dog and is wandering in the territory in which all of these other men have disappeared, when he comes to a lake. All of a sudden he sees a big hand come out of the lake. The hand is made of iron, it's rusty, and it grabs the dog and pulls it in. The hunter observes this, thinks about it very rationally, and then goes back and gets all the men in town to go out to the lake with buckets. Together, they take all the water out of the lake, and there at the bottom is a giant, rusted Iron Man— fifteen feet tall, with hair from his head all the way down to his ankles. The men capture him and bring him to the king, and the Iron Man is imprisoned in a big cage in the courtyard.

Now the king has a young son. One day when the son is out playing with a golden ball, throwing it around, he drops it and the golden ball rolls into the cage with the Iron Man. So, the Iron Man, with hair all the way down to his ankles, says to the little boy, "Do you want your ball back?" The boy says, "Yeah," and the Iron Man says, "Well then, you have to come in the cage with me."

The little boy gets scared and runs away crying, but he wants his ball back so he comes the next day and again says, "Can I have my ball back?" The Iron Man says, "You have to come in here with me if you want it." The boy says, "Well, I can't get in through the bars and I don't have the key." The Iron Man says, "I know where the key is. It's under your mother's pillow."

Finally, on a day when his mother and father are out, the boy decides to get the key. Then, he opens the cage. The Iron Man gives him the ball, walks out and starts to leave the castle. But the boy says, "You can't leave, because if my mother and father come back and find I've let you out, they'll kill me." So the Iron Man says, "Well, the only alternative, if you don't want to get in trouble with your mother and father, is to come with me." The little boy agrees and the Iron Man hoists him up onto his shoulders and off they go, together.

Bly explains the myth in terms of what is missing in today's men. The young boy playing with the golden ball is a common symbol in fairy tales. The golden ball symbolizes the innocence, spontaneity and freedom of youth, of children. The Iron Man, with hair down to his ankles, symbolizes the essence of a man—which is strong and can be violent when needed, animalistic, and organically powerful. But when the Iron Man confronts the child, he's not dangerous. They become good friends. He talks to the child. He doesn't hurt him, but he does take the child away from mommy and daddy. As a friend, the child rides on the Iron Man's shoulders. Bly's explanation goes on quite a bit from there but we needn't cover all of it for the purposes of this particular discussion.

If a man looks into the quality of masculinity of the Iron Man, it can be very scary. It is the quality of the primal man, the warrior, and is not only powerful and dynamic, but dark and ancient. When a man sees that, he says, "I shouldn't be that way. I shouldn't be aggressive, dominating, bestial. I should be soft, emoting all the time," and so on. He may deny that part of his masculinity to the point of complete suppression. Then, not only is it not dealt with, but he also doesn't have any energy.

Someone in touch with the Iron Man has a certain kind of energy. Maybe he's just a beast, an animal. It may be that the Iron Man is "running" him, and there is no wisdom, no overview. (There are lots of men around who are just animals, but they also have a certain intensity of energy.) Being in touch with the Iron Man also may mean that a man has dealt with that deep aspect of his masculinity and has recognized how it needs to be expressed. It must be expressed in some way for a man to be truly healthy. It needn't be expressed by being Mr. Macho—slapping women around and demeaning them; but, a man needs to recognize that the warrior, the ancient warrior, is one of the essential, primary qualities of masculinity in all men and that it cannot, or should not, be ignored. (And the primal quality of the feminine is the Mother; receptiveness.)

If a man doesn't deal with this essential masculine quality, basically he's castrating himself. He may develop tremendous qualities of softness, understanding, support and generosity, but something's missing—something very serious. Sooner or later what is missing is going to eat up the people whom the man is with—mate, friends, children. He will eat them up in an intuitive attempt to get from them this energy that he does not have.

It's a scary thing to confront that animal, because it's capable of such wild violence. And who can stop the Iron Man? The Iron Man devours people. But if you make friends with "it," allow it freedom, and trust it...it will never hurt anyone maliciously. It will function in a way that is the warrior.

Of course the Iron Man is not invulnerable. You know he's not invulnerable because of how he befriended the child. He ate all the hunters, for he meets aggression with its kind, but he befriended the child. He gave the boy back his ball, hoisted him up on his shoulders, and said he could come with him.

Bly gives the example of primitive cultures, like the Hopi Indian culture, in which, when a boy is twelve or thirteen years old, he is taken down into the *kiva*[2]. He stays there for a long period of time with the braves, and he doesn't see his mother for a year and a half. Even when he comes out of the *kiva*, he doesn't see his mother. This right of passage serves in part to sever whatever unhealthy aspects of mother-son bonding might have developed up till then.

Today, Bly says, when a child goes into the office with his father, and sees his father pushing papers instead of hunting, he can't understand how that's useful. Boys grow up having this tremendous conflict—feeling their fathers are useless. But when societies are work-oriented, as they were hundreds of

---

2   kiva - a large chamber in a Pueblo Indian village, often wholly or partly underground, used for religious ceremonies and other purposes.

years ago, and boys saw their fathers working the land or repairing a fence, then they developed pride. They realized that what their fathers did served something. Nowadays, a child doesn't understand how writing things on a piece of paper is useful work. A child may understand intellectually, but somewhere deep in his instinct, in his body, he feels confused and disoriented.

In many primitive cultures, when boys are twelve or thirteen years old, they are taken out of the feminine culture. They are sent out to hunt. There are always very profound initiatory rites for men (and many times for women also) into adulthood.

In one culture, the men would take the boys, and for three days they would isolate them with no food and no drink. Then they would bring them into the circle of all the men in the tribe. For three days, the boy had hardly slept and had no food, so he wondered what was going on. He had been alone with both his fears and his anticipation of manhood. But once he was brought to the circle of men, there was music and the air was charged, alive. Then all the men would whip out a knife, and one by one cut their arms, drip a little blood into a bowl, and give it to the boy to drink. They encouraged him to drink it, but they were not harsh or demanding. They encouraged him to drink in a soft and supportive way. It gave him the idea that all his life he'd been suckled by his mother, but now it was time to move into another domain, into a different relationship to her. It gave him the idea that the men could provide another type of food. It was a whole symbolic ritual they went through, which was very profound. A thirteen-year-old came out a man.

Bly suggested, however, that we don't have a men's culture in the modern day world, especially in the West. There are not even remnants.

Secret 38: Stay in Touch With The Streets

If a man surrenders to the Feminine without clear intention[3] and wisdom, then he's completely sucked into nothingness, into the soup of creation undefined by knowledge and consciousness. If, in his attempts to surrender to the Feminine, a man totally surrenders to "a" woman blindly, he gets to be a gigantic baby—either a needy, petulant, demanding child, or just an emotional vegetable. This can turn out to be fairly life-negative—very self-indulgent and insensitive. But if the Feminine can be surrendered to with clarity and wisdom, then it can be totally appreciated for what it is essentially, and therefore responded to and worshipped both in its true form and in the objective form of real adoration.

How does a man develop this clarity? By staying in touch with "the streets." Woman is not enough to entirely "feed" man—not ultimately. A man's own feminine needs to be perfected by his staying in touch with the streets. And for a men's culture to fully work, there has to be this organic and articulate understanding.

How have the Bauls historically stayed in touch with the streets? Literally, they wandered in the streets, got drunk, got

---

3   intention - commonly refers to the act of determining, mentally, some object or result. In Mr. Lee's work it is frequently used to mean having purpose in regard to one's work, or holding a wish for the Teaching to be true in oneself, or a wish to serve the Work. Intention may attract circumstances or opportunities for work, which cannot be self or ego-created.

laid, ate anything and everything and wrote poetry and song. Their singing and music were a result of their staying in touch with the streets and making friends with entities (energy forces) there. Their concept of communion with the Feminine was what developed from the "on-the-edge" living that being on the streets gave them.

If one is "on the streets" he better be able to pay attention and to discriminate. Naivete is not recommended. If you're doing something dangerous, like race-car-driving or mountain-climbing, you'd better have clear and defined priorities about your attention. Driving in Germany on the autobahn, for instance, at one hundred miles an hour, you can't take your eyes off the road for a fraction of a second. People whiz by at 130, 140, 150 miles an hour. You can't daydream when you're driving at one hundred miles an hour!

When you've been "on the streets," even in a minor way, you know that there's a certain edge that must be maintained or it's disaster. You need clarity and discrimination, not suspicion and braggadocio. In the movies, for example, the criminals always seem to know who is a policeman and who isn't, because criminals have clear, on-the-edge instincts. That instinct is pragmatic and enlivening, not useless psychological bullshit. That kind of instinct requires that you be really present.

When you have that presence, and you understand the need to embrace Woman, the Feminine, then in your interaction with this Force (whether it be with woman individualized or with the Feminine as a pole of energy, and whether you are a man or a woman), you aren't in danger of being swallowed up. For the Feminine *will* devour everything it can—completely. This is its nature—to subsume everything in its own evolutionary progression. If a man has clarity about his own femininity, he won't be endangered in a relationship by the "swallowing-up everything-in-its-path" machine, which the Feminine is always in danger of becoming when it is misconstrued by the "little feminine," the woman's psychology.

A woman needs to respond to her own Feminine with equal clarity so she doesn't become a "smothering machine": an empty ambulatory humanoid motored by crass sentimentality. With this lack of clarity the woman will just martyr herself, all the time, without distinction and appropriateness. For this type of woman it doesn't matter what's needed, what's wanted, who the person is, or what the situation is. You've seen what that can do to any environment, have you not? So, a woman needs to develop clarity as well as a man does. How does a woman develop this? Through the involvement in and response to women's culture—from the personal intimacy of friendship with other women. But a man will rarely get that clarity in a men's culture, for a men's culture has a different aim, a different goal. A man needs to get this clarity from the streets.

A lot of women these days are trying to get it from the streets too, and what that does is feed their masculinity and their delusions, not their femininity. Some women use the streets like a shot of testosterone. Literally, it's like making themselves men. This should be a source of great terror in men because it signals inaccessibility of the Feminine in such a woman. It's not that women should never skydive or practice fencing, for example, but they should be Woman before they skydive, so that when a certain kind of clarity arises, they don't allow it to generate an unnecessary masculine matrix. In a healthy woman there is a necessary element that her masculine aspect provides, but it's the indulgence, abuse, and dramatic exaggerations of this Masculine in any individual woman that creates such dissonance and disease.

Probably the most successful women who have not indulged or exaggerated the Masculine while still staying on the streets have been performers. In the performing arts a woman has got to be a woman. It's clear. In the performing arts, men and women are very distinct. In skydiving, they are not. It's not like there is polarized skydiving. But in the performing arts it's very clear, particularly in movies and in theater. Theater is designed with masculine and feminine roles. In something that is not designed with masculine and feminine roles, like race-car driving, sky-diving and rappelling, it is much more difficult for a woman to maintain a defined polarization as a woman, energetically speaking.

If a male culture is clearly defined and consistent, therapy groups are not needed every week. If there isn't a defined male culture, a men's support system should consider what it is to be in touch with the streets (and actually *be* in touch with the streets) so that a clear observation of what food that provides and what kind of clarity that generates is obvious to the men. Any martial art that involves competition is one way to effect that, even one that doesn't involve competition for prizes. Judo is an excellent one, because it's not a hard form, but the competition is still acute. Aikido is another.

Men and women can become very mature and satisfied with the food that their respective cultures provide, but without that exacting quality of clarity for a woman and for a man, sooner or later the culture may become sustaining and supporting, but will lose its true alchemical properties. If that element is present, then the cultures become vehicles for greater and greater transcendence, or greater and greater ecstasy, because then all the necessary nutrients are there for proper transformation.

Secret 39: What Women Want From Men

When a woman looks at a man there are two things she is attracted to. One is animal manliness or virility, and that's great for a while but it never lasts if the deeper elements of relationship are not satisfied. The value or heat of virility always gives way to frustration, emotional conflict, and rage. It never lasts as something that entirely fulfills a woman's needs, unless of course the people in the relationship remain as unconscious and insensitive as stones. To a woman with any sensitivity, virility may be attractive but it's not enough of a basis on which to find the depths of her essential Feminine Being.

So, what is enough? A man who is sensitive? A man who is able to express emotions? A man who respects the woman's feelings? Men like that are usually insecure and wimpy, having become more disassociated from their own masculinity than is healthy. After a while that sensitivity and emotional expression is not enough for a woman either. Soon she will need his essential Man-ness as a pole to her essential Woman-ness. So, the second thing that a woman is attracted to is genuine vulnerability—which in my terminology is the expression of Organic Innocence. What is it in a man that inspires truly profound love in a woman? Devotion—the devotion that arises out of a true and solid ground of masculine Presence, and inherence in Organic Innocence.

In the human kingdom there is no real surrender without devotion. A man cannot surrender unless he is a Man. If a man is insecure and vain he can't possibly surrender or express devotion in innocence. A woman instinctually knows that a man who can surrender is a man who can give her what she needs as a woman. (That is not the same as what she neurotically wants. A man who can fully surrender is not someone a woman can territorialize and control.)

Without a solid men's culture, this Teaching of true Surrender to the Will of God cannot make a difference in the world. In fact, it cannot even gain a small foothold.

So, the key to women's culture (and incidently to children's culture as well) is men's culture. It is crucial that men's culture be texturally appropriate so that women's culture can have the necessary and true dynamic to polarize toward. Then children's culture can be at the effect of and the reflection of the maturity of the adult culture. This would thus begin a cycle of mature, holy growth and education, free of the desperate struggles of childish and adolescent egos which try to override the demands of true and natural adult realities. That is how enlightened culture has to manifest.

Secret 40: The 90% Solution

Often, men will say or feel that they "can't live without a woman." And this tension could be both a neurotic obsession and the result of the intuitive recognition of what feminine energy is.

None of us would be alive without feminine energy, without "the Feminine." Relationship itself would not be a dynamic were it not for the qualities of the Feminine as a polar force of the Universe. Because we haven't grown up in a culture that understands these things, however, we typically tend to transpose our literal need for "the Feminine" onto a belief that we need a mate, a sexual partner. We turn the emptiness of our relationship to our *anima* (inner feminine in men) outward, and seek sex or mothering. In fact, this drive is often so consuming that we fail to develop deep and lasting friendships out of the obsession for codependent coupling. This is a great tragedy.

"The Feminine" is not exclusively present in only one individual. If a man thinks that a specific woman is the only source of feminine energy for him, and because he knows intuitively that without feminine energy he dies—spiritually and soulfully—there's always going to be tension when he's with the woman who is the specific attraction for him at the time. The woman means life just like breath means life, and there's always tension if one feels that he may not be able to continue to breathe.

The essential male aspect of creation is idea, pure intellect; and the feminine aspect of creation is form. The texture of this universe, therefore, is female.

Men can only become men by embodying, as a man, what is feminine—which is manifestation, energy, creation. Men have to become 90% Woman: man needs to embody, as a man, what this universe is essentially, which is Feminine. (Add the 90%-Woman to what a man already is, and then a man becomes a Man. Men have to become Men, but women are already Women, because basically we live in a feminine universe.)

The feminine aspect has certain characteristics having to do with receptivity, nurturing, feeling. In the domain of idea, there is no feeling. It doesn't exist. To become female, then, is to embody the feminine qualities—which is not just bodily feeling, like physical pain ("Ouch"), but a certain kind of feeling that generates nurturing and consideration.

What is so difficult about developing a men's culture is that when feeling arises, it wants to be nurturing and receptive, but it's almost a foreign trait to most men. Men would rather be competitive, and competition doesn't involve nurturing.

While feelings are only a piece of the feminine quality, *feeling* is actually the matrix of it. If you *feel* in a certain way, you will automatically be moved to manifest the other qualities. If you are only animating nurturing, however, your manifestation can be completely lopsided. If you animate *feeling* you can't be lopsided because *feeling* generates all the other things out of itself. If you animate nurturing, it doesn't necessarily generate the other qualities out of itself. The other qualities could be very one-sided, but *feeling* sources all of them. *Feeling* is really the key.

Secret 41: Essential Femininity and Essential Masculinity

Basically, there are two ways that Woman, the Essential Feminine, will be, and two ways the Essential Masculine, or Man, will be. Let's talk about the Woman first.

Woman, in the first way, will be deeply responsible for her essential Femininity, or for the Goddess. She will be profoundly strong, passionate, vibrant, hot and juicy. And this may well appear arrogant to anyone who doesn't sense her inner qualities. Even if she did not "get laid" for five years, even ten years, for example, this type of woman could still look bright, alive, and radiant every single day.

Any woman who is minimally in touch with her true being knows what I'm describing. She knows that look in herself, and so do men. It is so profoundly powerful and bright that it would scare any man completely out of his wits—except a fool, an animal, or a real Man (and even he would be stopped in his tracks, at least).

In English, unlike Sanskrit and other languages, the words, necessary inflections, or appropriate subtleties do not exist to describe who or what Woman is. Our culture is mute and narrow when it comes to the Real elements of Life and Ecstasy.

For the true Feminine to be real, it has to be founded upon one's inherent and spiritually organic power as Woman, not upon artificial appearances. When this is true of a woman, she needn't necessarily look fierce or angry, but she will appear wild. And that kind of wildness rests profoundly in one's essence as Woman, as Femininity or Shakti itself (Herself). That look cannot, even in one cell in a woman's body, be a response, a reflection of, or a consideration over and against anything else but Femininity. It cannot be false or neurotic. If one is concerned at all with the "other," other women or other men, with the illusion of separation and the drive to survive exclusively as the organic personality complex, it is impossible for that look to be Real, to come from "being."

Clothes, make-up, and seductive behavior "...do not a woman make." This knowing, feeling, and being Woman can have no masculine reference, i.e. no wanting to be "Woman" either because she wants to attract a man, or because she doesn't need a man. In the wealthy, militant feminist movement, for instance, a look of feisty self-assurance, although without the corresponding being, is very common. So too is its opposite—to be dressed down, with the look of self-deprecating, "I-couldn't-care-less," adolescent rebelliousness. (Then, whenever the woman wants, she can get all done up—with make-up, new clothes, lots of jewelry...) Poor feminists don't look that way, since that look tends to depend on having a lot of money.

Lots of women today appear to look self-confident, but that is because they're the boss. Perhaps they have fourteen men working under them in their department; they call the shots; they hire and fire; and they make $60-70,000 a year when the men are only making $30,000. It's the "stock-brokeress look" of one who's got more accounts than any of the men in the office, or of one who pulls the same "rank" at home. This is a look of pride in achievement, a pride in outdoing the patriarchy, but not a look of the Essential Feminine.

Women today are not willing to be women in relationship to their men. They are not willing to nurture, receive, live and generate attention, confidence, strength and power. Actually, there aren't many women around today. There are a lot of female bodies trying to be equal to men in masculine energy even though this approach wears the mask of wanting legal, moral, and economic equality.

In archetypal form, the man is the hunter and the woman is the hearth-keeper, the priestess, and lots of other things. But essentially, the man is the hunter and the woman provides an entire culture and environment. Shiva doesn't do anything; he sits on his meditation pillow or lotus bud and talks about truth. Shakti does everything—makes the home, provides the culture, circumstance, and inspiration.

Shakti is everything. But, women are not relaxing into being everything, they are trying to rule men. Today, women have a tremendous amount of conscious sexuality. And, among men, there is a greater incidence of impotence, more than ever before in history, because men are terrified of this energy in women. The women are saying, "I want to be on top," but they don't just mean in the sexual position; they mean all of it!

Consciousness-raising groups don't understand that the real way for women to handle this potent sexuality, this great abundance of energy, is to "give in so as to conquer." If you want to really run a man, give in. Don't come across like, "If you don't make me 'come' this time, forget it, Mac."

Give in, and the guy is helpless. Surrender to him, and you can do and expect anything—even miracles.

"Give in so as to conquer" is the principle in judo, and also the principle in "winning." If you really want to win, if you really want to master a situation, you have to give in and allow that situation itself to transcend its own limitations and resistances. It will, if you apply this principle properly.

Overpowering everything is not the way. The way to win or master a situation is through ruthless softness and uncompromising gentleness. The women who did that best in the annals of history are the women who had real power. Women who could humble the greatest poets, the greatest writers, and the greatest warriors were women who knew how to "give in so as to conquer."

It's perfectly true, as chauvinistic as it may sound. Women have to be willing to recognize, in a completely non-arrogant and receptive way, that they are the power behind the throne. They need to know this tacitly and essentially, not egotistically. After all, it is obvious, organically obvious.

But, instead of being content to be the power behind the throne, women want to sit on the throne, and that is where the problem comes in. That's what is going on today.

Particularly in the western world, men are basically ciphers of their mothers. There are so few men today who can be viewed as role models. Men don't know what their masculinity is. They want to be the power behind the throne! Instead of realizing that they are not, they go around perpetuating violence against women.

Men have to be willing to recognize that Woman is the power behind the throne, and to honor that through worship. That's not the same as saying, "Yes, I'll vote for the Equal Rights Amendment." This is a private consideration, an intimate affair, not a public, political consideration.

Women have to be worshipped. Without feminine energy there would be no creation.

The "huntress" too is a genuine archetype of the essential feminine; it is *just* fierce, but it is not out to "get" anyone in particular. The fierceness of the archetypal huntress is universal: it is fierceness towards sloth, towards illusion, towards doubt, confusion, and ignorance of the feminine. Fierceness that is vindictive, personal, racial, or prideful, however, is characteristic of a huntress-look that is impure, or neurotic.

Women who are resting in their essence as a Woman might look one of two ways. The first type, for instance, might sleep sprawled out on the bed with her legs spread and her arms flopped to the side. Women who look that way wouldn't worry themselves to sleep, or stay awake because of stress or tension. They wouldn't sleep curled up in a fetal position or with their legs crossed and their arms over their breasts, all cool and contained.

The other way Woman could look, or be, is completely soft, round, quiet, with no harsh edges—in her voice, in her body, in her eyes, or in her gestures. That softness is from the absorption of attention in the Personal God, in the Prayer of Submission and Love. Such a woman's energy would be more internalized than externalized.

Woman, Real Woman, will either be radiating outwardly, towards the world, towards the known and unknown Universe, or radiating inwardly. She would not radiate towards herself because in Real Woman there is no "herself" except as a convenience of language and communication. Neither will she cease to be functional. Rather, the Woman who radiates inwardly will appear more of a hearthholder than a warrior.

Neither type is better than the other type. They are simply different in manifestation. (In the more outwardly-oriented Woman, her contextual or essential focus is not defined by "God only," but by "Only-God." The distinction is that "God-only" is the Immanent aspect of the Absolute[4] and "Only-God" is the Transcendental aspect of the Absolute.[5])

Looking one of those two ways in form only can be an act, either conscious or subconscious, devious or naive, in order for a woman to get what she wants. Some women look soft, retiring and very sweet, and yet they've got claws sharper than any tiger. Anything in between those two ways of being Woman is a function of neurosis. Such an intermediate way might carry some degree of transformational affect or possibility, but it is

---

4 Immanent aspect of the Absolute - the personal God; the God as recognized in and through creation.

5 Transcendental aspect of the Absolute - The non-personal all-pervasive universal principle of Creation which is beyond human comprehension, and beyond description.

still unfinished, blocked, or thwarted in its expression. There are no exceptions. If a woman wants to be "equal" to a man and live in a "man's world," then neither of these two ways of being Woman can be real for her. There is no equality except in the Divine sense. Man is not Woman and Woman is not Man and never will be.

Complete submission to the *yin* quality of receptivity will either manifest as completely receptive or completely wild Shakti. Neither one excludes the other, of course, and both types will have a wide range of manifestations when necessary, and under various circumstances.

• • •

In order for Woman to be able to walk around animating one of these two ways of being and not be molested all the time (I don't mean jumped on and physically molested, but psychically and emotionally molested), Man has to be either one of two ways. One of the essential ways Man can look and be is completely clear.

When one looks into a man's eyes one can always tell when there's a deep being—one who is free to live within his own masculinity. Eyes are either clear or cloudy. (I don't mean the color of the irises or the whites. Everyone knows the difference; everyone has looked at a lot of eyes.) Clear eyes sparkle; clear eyes are bright and bottomless. There's no film over or in those eyes and that manifests in an upright posture, and a refusal to leer at women, among other things.

Some men look elegant no matter what they are wearing because they have a clarity of context. In an interview recently, an older male movie-star was asked, "Are you really attractive to women? In your last movie you looked so old and dumpy, tired and dragged out..." He said, "Yes, of course, I'm attractive to women. Women don't like these guys who bounce around on the beach and have nothing in between their ears. They like somebody who knows who he is. And," he said, "I know who I am. That's attractive no matter what I look like."

That quote points to the beingness of Man, not just to some superficial self-confidence. When a man knows who he is in the context of masculinity, he carries himself with a certain kind of elegance. The natural beingness of a Man is to carry himself with the elegance of a warrior chief who knows he's a warrior chief. He is just that, without "posturing" or "posing."

The other way Man could show up is as invisible. Invisibility carries with itself an unmistakable elegance that most people never recognize. (They're too busy looking for the "Emperor's new clothes.") Invisibility is the ability to naturally and spontaneously integrate oneself into any environment as if one belonged there—to be a human chameleon. It's rare to find this type of man because the psychology of the male "primate"—the chest-beating, teeth-bearing ape—is convinced that such invisibility is weak and "unmanly." But this softness in Man is the counterpart to the softness in Woman. Such a man worships the Goddess inside, while the more outward type of man dramatizes "Only-God."

To worship the Goddess in such a way is to be soft to Her Demand and Her Power, and to yield to Her. It doesn't mean that the more "sparkling" type of man doesn't respond to the Goddess, but that his focus is more universal than personal.

Once one has gotten a sense of his or her essential beingness as Man or Woman, one should not be insecure or confused over it.

Let me clarify this language. It's not that Woman could be Real in these ways and Man could be Real in these ways. No. Those descriptions actually define true Femininity and true Masculinity. These ways are not something you can "try" to be; they are what you discover to be your true self. You then relax into your essential condition as weights and distractions get sloughed off by your observation of their irrelevance to True Being.

Secret 42: Becoming Woman

I. FOR MEN:

Man discovers the Feminine within himself by "becoming Woman." It's not by becoming "a woman," dressing like a woman and acting like a woman, although those forms of serious sadhana have produced transformative manifestations in many men. To *become Woman* is a very different process, however.

A simple way to begin to figure out how to do that is to observe Woman. Now if you look at women and try to find Woman, typically you're going to have to ignore a lot of drama and appearance. For a man to observe women, he has to be very clear about the difference between essential femininity and "primate" female behavior. Nevertheless that is where the role model is.

If you look at a woman's outer behavior, and that behavior is shaped by the contemporary, frustrated, independent, "we're equal-with-men" mode of expression, you may miss the whole thing. In order to understand what "becoming Woman" is, you have to observe what is of value when that conditioned disposition is not in effect. In other words, you have to notice what is real, rather than what is just a psychological affectation. If you get the chance to observe women doing their toilet, that's a situation in which this conditioned disposition tends to be relaxed. A woman tends to be closer to who she really is when she is looking in the mirror.

You start by observing women and reading between the lines, so that you begin to sense the essence of femininity, rather than training, habit, or cultural expectation.

It's much easier for a man to become Woman than for a woman to become Woman; a woman thinks she already is Woman, when she's only "a woman." It's much more difficult for a woman, because she has to surrender to what she already is—like the proverbial fish in the ocean being thirsty. All a man has to do is see Woman in women, and allow that to incorporate itself in his own being, from within. It's like getting a contact "hit."

• • •

The Feminine will teach you to dance if you don't know how. It's not a crime for a man to let the woman lead until he learns to lead. How's a man going to learn to lead except by learning from a woman? In terms of our discussion it's not "a woman"— it's Woman, the Feminine. Let the Feminine (whatever that is) provide the lessons in dance, provide the example, not by making any one woman an example, not by watching "a" woman. The Feminine will teach you to dance. She is a dancer.

Investigate how the feminine quality apples to any given situation, and what the essential mood of the feminine is. The mood is not the form it tends to manifest as, such as comfort, nurturing, mothering, receptivity. That form is not necessarily the dance. But there's a mood of receptivity and a mood of mothering, and a mood of nurturing that *is* the dance. It's not the act that's the dance, it's the mood.

II. FOR WOMEN:

There are many differences, and of course a few similarities, between the quality of nurturing that is called for between a mother and a child, and the quality of receptivity and response that is appropriate between a woman and her mate. One of the ways a woman begins a consideration of the differences is to ask her mate if he thinks she "mothers" him. His response will be an accurate assessment of whether there is imbalance in this particular type of love.

156

Men tend to be very, very touchy about such issues, however, since few have been mothered properly. Therefore, to consider this issue seriously, a woman needs to dispose herself not to recoil from the cynicism of men.

Women should consider, not "What is a mother...what is a lover...what is a hearth-keeper...a homemaker...?" but rather, "What is Woman?" The question should not be, "What is a woman?". A woman is just a bundle of psychological motivations and personality traits with a subtle core-essence that has a polar relationship to the subtle core-essence of the masculine. (A woman is just like a man is these things, only his polar energy is in relationship to the feminine.)

When a woman finds out who she is, she just finds out that she likes Chinese food better than Indian food, and that she prefers to be on top instead of on the bottom during intimate moments...and so on. When a woman discovers who she is as Woman, she discovers a creature of a different sort.

There is a quality of feminine energy which, when freed from psychological expectations, projections, and aberrations is spontaneously responsive to any given circumstance as Woman, as The Feminine, not as defined by any particular role that a woman may assume.

The first thing to do in considering the question "What is Woman?", is to be very specific about the language. Whenever you think about it—with all the extrapolations, implications, and distractions that can be involved—always think of it as, "What is Woman?" Don't get sloppy. Always be very exacting. A minor or seemingly insignificant change in language can make a major difference in the outcome.

Secondly, an interesting experiment would be to ask a lot of women that same question: "What is Woman?" When they say, "Well, you know a mother...and a this and a that...," you say, "No, no, not what is a woman. What is Woman?"

If you're willing to take a large sampling, you'll find most of the answers useless. But, every once in a while, somebody will slip; her personality will relax for a moment, and then you'll get a response that's absolutely priceless—a revelatory gem that can be food or fuel for years, or lifetimes, or...oh hell let's go for it...even forever! But, be prepared to receive such an answer to this question in whatever form it comes. It would be very unusual for it to come in a verbal way. You'll have to be able to "feel through" the words that are being spoken into the heart and soul of who is answering.

When a woman finds out what Woman is, that revelation will transcend all personal characteristics and all self-absorptive, self-referencing expressions.

III. FOR MEN AND WOMEN:

What it is to be Woman has got no name. To be Woman has got no "I." Woman is receptivity, essentially, and receptivity has no "I." It embraces; it doesn't confront.

Everything with an "I" confronts: "I'm this, I'm that. I'm part of the relationship. I cook your meals. I deserve better than this." (Pop psychology in the women's movement is about deserving your seventeen orgasms. It begins with, "You deserve at least one, and once you've had one, honey, there's no limit...You deserve to be treated properly, etc., etc., etc." Assertiveness training, or anything that has a big "I" in it, is not receptive. To be essentially receptive is to be without "I.")

Whenever I talk about this, women say that if you try to be that way with a man, he will walk all over you. Well, what about that? You can't keep putting up with being treated like shit forever and ever. It's a valid argument. What to do?

First of all, if you are going to be a Real Woman you need to have "something" to meet that Real Woman. You need something to embrace—like a Real Man—if you try to be completely surrendered to receptivity.

Secondly, these ideas need to be considered directly in the circumstance in which they apply. Right now, we're not making love. We are creating the question, "What is a Real Woman?" Or, "How do I become a Real Man in order to meet this Real Woman?" Those questions are most appropriately asked when you are in the proper chamber, for instance the next time you are making love, whether in the sexual or non-sexual domain. (I'm talking specifically about lovemaking, but not about "rutting" in the biological sense.) You can apply lovemaking to being with a child, or to being in communion with friends, although of course there are differences.

Do not look for techniques to manage your energy, but simply make this consideration in the moment it applies. This question should be held interiorly, then it will pop up when it has some relevancy. If you make this consideration properly you will be doing what the consideration is about. It's very simple—black and white.

That is all it is useful for me to say about this subject, at this time. Too many spices ruin the stew. Anything that we genuinely want to realize for ourselves must be left as a question...as a *koan,* as they say in Zen. If a pre-digested answer is given to a question of that importance, you are left with something very unnatural. We're not built to eat pre-digested food. We're built to eat, to digest food, and then to shit, which is a very important part of the process. If you don't do that, you're in big trouble.

If one uses Woman as the *koan,* then when the process of becoming Woman begins to take effect, the chakras will naturally and spontaneously align without unusually disruptive influences, as described in many yoga treatises. This whole process will not need extraordinary attention, adjustment, or refining.

You can approach becoming Woman by beginning to work with aligning the chakra systems, but, when you approach that knowledge through willful intention, you will, when you reach completion, have to give up the willful intentional process that brought you to completion. Then, it gets done all over again for you.

If one discovers Woman, he will automatically discover Man. It's really a simultaneous realization because these polarities do not exist separate from one another even though distinctions can be pointed at.

The task—becoming Woman—is exactly the same for all men and all women, only the purpose is different. But, there isn't any "way" to surrender to Woman inside of oneself because it isn't a linear or progressive process. There's just doing it. That's why it's a *koan*. You work with it and work with it...and one day, there it is—accessible and true of you.

The purpose of man and woman in each seeking Woman is different because man and woman represent different polarities. So, you might ask: "Why should Woman not seek for Man?"...And I would answer: Woman is everything. What does she need to seek Man for?

Secret 43: Women's Psychological
Response to Male Weakness

For any relationship to work there will always be the play of opposites—male-female, yin-yang, positive-negative, or affirming-denying forces. If two people are so alike that this ebb/flow-pattern of universal creation does not exist, then a force outside of the couple such as a social or political cause, a religion, or a life circumstance, must serve that function.

Men enter relationships almost exclusively as the weaker force of the two. (If you pay attention, men, you will see that probably every woman you have ever met has actually been the dominant force; and if you pay attention, women, you will see that you've always been this way in relationship to men—as the dominant force to their submissive or weak force.)

If there is no consciousness or self-reflection, women will respond primally to that weakness—from the psychological relationship of unawakened man/woman dispositions; from neurotic rather than pure motives; from a sub-conscious mood that the relationship has already failed, instead of that the relationship is an open field with infinite possibilities.

Instinctually, what is wanted in a relationship is the natural interplay of essential masculine and essential feminine energy. But, if a man does not express true masculinity, which is what women want, a woman will typically not respond with true femininity. Rather, she will respond with a neurotic or mechanical psychological reaction to the man's neurotic or mechanical psychology. And her response will be primal, unconscious, and functioning all the time as an underlying mood, even when it isn't generating outward signs. The only time that response will not be present will be when a man expresses true masculine energy. But this will only come from a woman who has some true sense of who she is as Woman, as the real feminine presence.

A primary difficulty of relationship is that once a woman has the habit of responding in a neurotic pattern, even if she finds a man who expresses true masculine energy, she will still attempt to run the same psychological games. A momentum develops which just goes on almost by its own power. She will run into extreme crisis because the Organic Innocence of her femininity recognizes the Organic Innocence of masculinity, yet there will be conflict between her attempt to commune with that, and her mechanical conditioning to "run" her primal psychological pattern. A woman doesn't learn this when she is ten years old. It's learned from infancy—from the minute she starts observing mommy and daddy.

That psychological response to men is, in general, so overwhelming that there is basically no room for surrender to that which allows the natural expression of the true Feminine.

How does a man work with that mechanism? It's impossible to stop it in any other way except transcending the behavior that elicits that response—and even that is just the first step. This means that men have to do their *sadhana* first, before they will ever be in a relationship that ultimately works spiritually. Men have to stop animating the weakness which elicits woman's primal psychological response to that weakness. Being a macho hero does not necessarily put an end to that weakness. As you all well know, some of the most macho men are also some of the weakest and most insecure. Often such dramatic bravado is just a smoke-screen for the true state of affairs. Real masculine strength is not sharp, harsh, steely-cold, cruel or brutal. It is masculine neurosis that sees it this way.

If a man stops manifesting the weaknesses of his failure to be Man, the woman will eventually stop responding over-whelmingly with the primal psychological mechanism of "the Sneer." When that is out of the way, the Organic Innocence of feminine energy, the essence of femininity is expressed. But, when this happens, a neurotic man can be so bowled over by the woman's brilliance that he gets even weaker, and then the whole damn thing can start all over. That's a very real possi-bility, so you have to be on your guard every second. A man must acknowledge and be able to stand in true Masculinity, at least to own it when it is there! It's a little tricky. We can talk about this now, but practically, all of that takes place after one begins to function from a disposition of "Draw No Conclusions Mind"[6] and awakened Context. Once men and women are able to express their masculinity and femininity through Organic Innocence, then one need not worry about sexuality. That does-n't mean there will be a big, wild orgy every night, where men and women melt into all the one another's in the room, although that is what you might think philosophically if you consider this image. The problems of sexuality, desire, lust, chemistry, fantasy, and so on simply become disposed to the instinctual nature of a life surrendered to the Will of God.

When a man enters a disposition of Essential Masculine, he has the possibility of ceasing to activate and manifest the usual weaknesses that he neurotically brings into relationship, which he only learned from his mother anyway. He learned it from his mother and had it verified by watching his father.

So, what kind of work can take place on a woman's part to help this unnatural situation? Well, to keep it simple—women should bring their attention to surrender, and men should bring their attention to sadhana. Later, the roles reverse. Men bring

---

6   Draw No Conclusions Mind - a state of clarity in which mental assumptions
     are surrendered in favor of Innocence; that is, the simple reality of the moment.

their attention to surrender and women bring their attention to *sadhana*. In one sense women have it easy, though, because their *sadhana* is done for them as long as the men do their part. As long as men don't start remanifesting that weakness, women aren't going to start remanifesting that primal psychological response, at least after a certain point of maturity of distinction, discipline and effort is reached.

Secret 44: Approach the Feminine Without Dominance

If one approaches knowledge of the Feminine from a masculine viewpoint, or from a context of "male-mindset," he or she will already have failed because the Feminine cannot be fooled or understood except in it's own "space." Sometimes the Feminine will go along with a misunderstanding or a mis-interpretation on the part of someone who is trying to grasp it for various reasons, but it will never be conned. If we are going to understand what the Feminine is, we have to approach from the perspective of what that is from inside, not from the obser-vations and perspective of a man, or from outside—which is always in some fashion a forceful perspective...the perspective of power and dominance.

Traditionally, patriarchal cultures would worship the gods for healthy and productive crops, for favorable weather, as well as for power, to win wars and to dominate their neighbors. The Goddess was worshipped for anything that had to do with life on a practical and essential level. Patriarchal cultures developed Goddess worship at a certain point in history as a forceful approach to the Feminine. "If she's not going to go away we might as well use her to our advantage."

What is the most forceful approach to the Feminine? Sex. In previous times cults full of priestesses developed, and these priestesses acted as temple prostitutes, usually once a year, but sometimes all the time. They were literally like the east-ern definition of the guru—they symbolized and were related to as if they were the Goddess incarnate. To fertilize the priestess, then, was to appease and please the Goddess. And if the Goddess was appeased, then she would smile on the culture which appeased her—there would be great crops, wars would be won, and everybody would be healthy.

It is interesting that the predominant Goddess cults in the "new age" today are demanding to be approached with that kind of force. Despite their rhetoric, they are demanding to be approached from the masculine perspective. The rhetoric is all feminine, feminine, feminine, but their behavior demands a masculine approach. The women in such processes are so divorced from their own true feminine that they don't even know what they are doing today. They have been conditioned by the masculine perspective and they superimpose this on their instinctual search for true Femininity. But such an approach can only produce some kind of aberration, and has.

This masculine approach is defined by making biased distinctions between the masculine and the feminine, demanding a certain type of recognition as "the feminine," and by rhetoric that's exclusive and righteous, or fundamental-specific.

Women have been abused by men for so long that they've lost the sense of who they are humanly, and who they are as Goddess. They need to reclaim that sense of who they are, essentially, for themselves—for their own confidence and pride. And this need has been the drive behind all popular culture feminism. However, obeisance to the true Feminine will come from gratitude and recognition on the part of the masculine (both in men and women), not from harsh demands.

When a man meets a woman, essentially his relationship to her is that of urgency and tension. Why? Sex! No matter how subtle or sophisticated the man is, sex is the bottom line. He too is absolutely trapped by an overwhelming social paradigm of woman-hatred. Why does a man want sex from a woman? What in that generates urgency and tension? The answer is:

man feels the neurotic and terrified need to dominate that which in fact is Life itself—or Shakti.

All sexual play that has orgasm as it's aim cannot be other than motivated by urgency and tension. When orgasm is why two people (or more) join...why they are making love, and when that is the ultimate fulfillment that can be imagined of that particular union, the higher possibilities of love and communion are denied. When a man approaches sex with the unconscious dynamic of urgency and tension, the motivating factor is dominance of the Feminine out of fear—terror actually of being not dominated by, but so surrendered to this Feminine as to become nothing in it's brilliance.

It is the same for women. The contemporary middle-class woman is not interested in real pleasure...in essential delight. It might not appear that way, because the rhetoric is all about how many orgasms a woman can have and about pleasing herself and getting full sensual satisfaction. But it's all a mask for denial and refusal.

This sensual satisfaction is a hot topic in popular psychology magazines and all the female magazines. "If your man can't satisfy you, dig the vibrator. It's better anyway and you can do it your way...no mess, no emotional fuss...or attachment." That's not about pleasure, it's about dominance. If women approach sex full of tension and urgency, then dominance is the underlying motive; though in a woman's case it is dominance over her own fear of her power and reality. A woman can be just as terrified of being that which she is, as a man is of becoming that (the Feminine) or surrendering into that.

Secret 45: The One and Only True Secret of Tantric Sex and God Forgive Me For Giving It away So Cheaply.

When a man and a woman meet in sex, there should only be one consideration. The man should essentially be asking the woman to show herself as Woman, and the woman should be asking the man to show himself as Man.

I don't mean asking verbally, or you will get all mixed up in philosophy and lose interest in the flesh at hand. This consideration, and occasionally procreation, is all that sex is really about. Sex as pleasure, or even sex as alchemy, is just a sophisticated way of animals trying to justify being in human form. The whole tantric consideration of sex as alchemy is the necessary mind-stuff to keep whoever is practicing it interested long enough to get the real "hit." For a man who is with a woman, the question...the gateway...the key to the universe is, "Show me Woman."

The whole process of tantric sexual work is to strip away from a woman all the things she thinks she is as a woman—all the artifices she has superimposed on top of raw, primal, feminine beingness. The same is true of a man. A woman should only have sex with a man when she has the vulnerable mood of wanting to be shown raw, primal masculinity.

The female tantric initiators of the old days knew how to get a man to that door. These female tantric masters knew how to strip away all the artifices, leaving a man to view not only what the real Feminine was but what the real Masculine was in himself. Initiation only came after years of apprenticeship work because if you get a man to that place, and he is not prepared for it, he is liable to crack. Really, he might just go insane, or be so terrified that he would never try anything like that again as long as he lived. He would never seek Real life.

Such initiation was nothing like what we know through superficial insight or intellectual study. Tantric work was to strip women and men of all the habitual psychological impositions on essential femininity and masculinity. That is what all sex should be. If it is anything else, if sex is a matter of ordinary love, it can only lead to disappointment and frustration, or to the perpetuation of unconsciousness. It has to be more than that.

When people are in love, sex can be the particular form of love that leads them to the revealing of the true Man and Woman in each. If it's just "prove that you love me...," it's got to end up in frustration. There is just no other way it can end up. (I shouldn't have even said this out loud. The only reason I did is because nobody will get it anyway...with one or two rare exceptions.)

The bottom line of all sexual relationships is, "Show me..." (That is different than some personality-based, anima-animus nonsense.) When a man is with a woman, sex should never be a matter of how many orgasms the woman has, or the look on her face, or whether she moans or screams.

For a lot of men, a half hour...45 minutes...an hour...and it's enough already. You've hunted the quarry, the deer is "bagged,"...then you get bored. The woman has had a couple of orgasms (or moaned and looked into your eyes like you are the greatest thing there ever was on the face of the earth), and then you become bored. If you can't hold the intention: "Show me

Woman," then basically, sex can be extraordinarily pleasurable and very fulfilling for a long time, but ultimately sex from that perspective has got to die.

For a man, the end is "Show me Woman." That's not, "Who are YOU as a woman?" Any woman, anyone born in the female sex, can show that. There might be some rare exceptions, but essentially it doesn't matter who she is, what she is built like, what her personality is like—women are all women. That is the point.

A real Woman wants to know who Man is, but other women do not. To know Man would defeat the average woman's psychic purposes—every one of them, including the movement toward family and love and so on.

Woman is a profound mystery. Most men have no interest in that. They want to get laid and get it over with. And every woman thinks if she just moans a little, she shows the guy who she is. No. A woman's consideration should be "Show me Man," not "I'll show you Woman." Lots of women think, "I'm going to show you who Woman is," but pretty soon they find out that they don't know their *yoni* from a hole in the ground.

"Show me Woman" could take years to get to...or you could get to it the first time out, or at least touch it the first time out. It depends on who you are and what you are doing.

A man who knows what this Work is will never be satisfied unless he somehow finds out what Woman is. Sex is not the only way, thank goodness. There are other ways. But sex is the least mysterious, most obvious way. This way has a sign—six feet high in red neon letters—pointing to it. The other ways are infinitely more subtle.

Basically, man should develop the tacit context of "Show me Woman," and then forget it. To talk about that to a woman is like asking her, "When are you going to 'come'?" That could really get someone self-conscious. (Nowadays, of course, most

170

women would say, "If you can't see it yourself, sucker, go find someone else.") By talking about it and not enquiring from a mood of "Show me...," the entire thing would be voided.

Take my word for it. Make this your *koan* and go for it. Try to develop some intensity behind wanting to know Woman, wanting to know Man.

Secret 46: Balancing The Essential Masculine and Feminine Energies

Within every human being there are masculine/feminine polarities, and there is a whole spectrum of the interplay of those energies—from almost completely masculine, to almost completely feminine, and all points in between. People are born with organic dispositions somewhere within that spectrum. Men and women have clear tendencies towards strong masculinity or strong femininity, irrespective of their actual gender. For instance, someone with a very strong feminine disposition, man or woman, could develop a very effective utilization, experience, or expression of masculine energy, but that wouldn't change his or her essential disposition.

Typically, when there is a recognition of the nature and relationship of male and female energy, there is an understanding that those energies are elemental in every aspect of creation, animate and inanimate. Some of the most dramatic classical music, for instance, is effective in its communication because of the play between masculine and feminine forces in the music itself. Some music is clearly masculine and some music is clearly feminine. Within that context, then, sexual activity becomes one way among many ways of utilizing the dynamic between masculine and feminine poles, whether in homosexuality or heterosexuality (there are obvious differences, but energy-wise, the same thing can apply). Sexual play becomes just one form of integrating and balancing the interplay between the masculine and feminine forces, and not necessarily the most meaningful or primary form.

Homosexuality is actually a relationship between a man and a woman—irrespective of the biological gender of the people involved in the homosexual relationship. Most male homosexuals would be seriously offended, I think, by the consideration that their homosexuality is actually a relationship between themselves and their biological mothers, rather than between them and the man they choose to have a relationship with. But, that is just the way it is, all offense aside.

This is not true of all homosexuals, and not all homosexuality is neurotic, but in the vast majority of cases, the choice to be homosexual is a reaction against some childhood trauma, abuse, or shame, not actually a choice for the same sex. When you consider how many primal habits of recoil were assumed early in your development, it should be psychologically clear that this is literally true.

In a homosexual relationship that "works—(the definition of "works" being a relationship that's based on love and natural attraction, not on neurotic psychological dynamics or avoidances), it's obvious that both male and female energies interplay in the relationship. It's not exclusively male energy in a male homosexual relationship, and female energy in a female homosexual relationship.

When one does not intuit or realize that male and female energy is the essential nature of the interplay between all forces in the universe (not just between men and women), then sex becomes the relationship that most dramatizes the interplay of energies. Whether it's a homosexual or a heterosexual relationship, it doesn't matter. This is obvious in a large section of any given homosexual community where there are tremendously feminine manifestations in some men, and tremendously masculine manifestations in some women. This is not an attempt by men to be women, or by women to be men, but a dramatization of the interplay between the masculine and feminine forces.

A friend of mine, who is a Teacher, once did an experiment. He invited a female impersonator to make up all the men in his community to look like women, and then asked the men to act like women throughout the afternoon. The women in the community were to observe the men, but not make any effort to interact with or impose themselves upon them.

At first, the men felt very uncomfortable and their way of dealing with the discomfort was to exaggerate how they thought women acted. They raised their voices and started to gesture in the way they thought women would gesture—the way women looked to them. But, after a while, that felt dissonant, so they finally stopped all their mimicry and started acting "normal"— the way they always did, except that now they were made up and dressed in women's clothing. Once they relaxed and allowed the exercise to take its normal course, they actually began to feel very much like a group of women.

At that point the Teacher told them to go take their make up off and get dressed in their usual clothes and to stop the exercise. (But, by that time they didn't want to!)

Later on, the women said that at first the men seemed like bizarre caricatures. But as soon as they stopped trying to act, the women felt like these "men" were just another group of women, and that they (the women) could be among them (the men) easily, like it was "just all us women..." Some of the men still had beards and moustaches, but it was as if they were invisible. It didn't make any difference.

When the men described their experience, it was with an air of wonder because they realized something very primal and essential—something transformative even.

One of the aspects of developing spiritually is recognizing what your born, natural disposition is; and not needing to dramatize, exaggerate, indulge or suppress that.

• • •

If someone has a weak feminine part and a stronger essential masculine, or a weak masculine and a stronger essential feminine, he or she will typically seek balance not through strengthening the weak part, but by reducing the strong part or developing habits which give the appearance of strength in the weak area. This may create the illusion of balance—the mind says, "Okay, now I'm in balance, I've done this difficult work." But actually, things are exactly the same as they always were.

The answer to this dilemma is quite simple. A weak masculine will be balanced by strengthening that masculine. Sometimes, however, the personality has developed in an overly masculine way as the body's compensation for weak essential masculinity. Then, one will have to work very hard to deal with the tenacity of those habits. The "act" of masculine manifestations keeps a person from realizing that such masculinity is hollow and insubstantial. If one strengthens the essential masculine, however, the personality will adjust as the body achieves balance. And since the body knows instinctively what healthy balance is, the individual won't have to do anything about it.

(If you've ever tried changing your personality, even very, very slightly, you'll know how extremely difficult it is. You need tremendous willpower even to look like you're being different, let alone to achieve lasting sustained change. But you're not really different if you're just acting different.)

Likewise, if you have an overdeveloped essential masculine and a weak feminine, you don't try to carve off some part of the masculine. You strengthen the essential feminine.

Some people understand that femininity is "receptive" and that masculinity is "active." This is both simplistic and not exactly accurate. It covers one facet of the whole picture, but not the essential masculine and feminine. If one wants the male/female energy balanced in the body, he or she must go directly to the essential masculine or feminine, which is very different than the superficial expressions.

In the essential male-female dichotomy, Shiva is pure knowledge, that is, Context. Shakti is content—manifestation, form, and energy. Shiva is unmanifested allness, and Shakti is everything else—everything sensual, alive, moving, created. A weak feminine, therefore, can be related to an element (in the whole body of psychological/emotional/physical ingredients) that has difficulty acting, doing, or manifesting. Shiva is the strong silent type, not the warrior. Diana, Athena, or Shakti is the warrior. You strengthen the feminine, therefore, by acting...of course in the proper way, not just flailing about making waves or crashing around like a bull in a china shop.

Masculine energy doesn't speak. It *is*. Feminine energy acts: it speaks; it is alive, aggressive and powerful. Masculine energy just radiates based on wisdom, not based on accomplishment or beauty. The way you strengthen a weak masculine is by resting in pure knowledge—by coming to know, to discover, wisdom. If you are insecure, if you think you don't know anything, the way to strengthen a weak masculine is to find that place in yourself that does know and acknowledge it, embrace it. Anytime you get this feeling that you don't understand, you immediately enquire, specifically in relationship to that insecurity.

To strengthen the feminine is to use your energy in an optimally productive fashion, not squander it and reenforce the weaknesses. That doesn't mean you can't take a walk, or sit in the park watching people, but that should be a way of feeding one's spiritual work, one's essential hungers, not an avoidance of one's deep being. A very practical way to strengthen the feminine through optimal activity is to never leave a project unfinished; another way is through conservation of energy in the use of speech.

To summarize, if the masculine is too weak, don't worry about whether the feminine is too strong or not. Strengthen the masculine. If the masculine is too strong, don't even pay any attention to it. Strengthen the feminine.

Secret 47: Beyond Male and Female

We need to be able to be a little flexible. The ideal is to be masculine or feminine as the situation calls for it, but very few people are flexible enough to be either masculine or feminine depending on circumstantial need. Some people in fact are terrified of it. Most men are pretty stuck on trying to be masculine, and can't be feminine even if the situation demands that, and most women try to be feminine and can't be masculine if the situation demands that.

In the act of sex, the man can be masculine or feminine and the woman can be feminine or masculine. When you approach sex with the idea that you can be Man or Woman, you can forget which one you are. You can just be the event that's going on, the interplay of instinctive energies. Orgasm becomes a losing proposition at that point, an energy suffocator. You can forget orgasm, because what you are doing is better. If you are into the energy interplay deeply, you forget whether you're a man or a woman and who you're doing what to. You're just into it. Being in *that,* far exceeds the momentary pleasure of orgasm, and you go on from there. Then delight transcends the "This is better" mood. Ecstasy subsumes the duality of coupling.

PART V

Tantra—Advanced Considerations

Beginning with an extensive treatment of the center / chakra system as a basis for understanding sexual energy in the process of human development, the author goes on to warn the casual xreader of the dangers of the Tantric path, and finally to elaborate upon the concept of Becoming Woman by introducing the exalted principle of the Adoration of Woman.

Secret 48: The Chakras and The Centers[1]

In yoga philosophy, the first chakra is the perineum, the second chakra is the genitals (sex center), the third chakra is the solar plexus, the fourth chakra is the heart, the fifth chakra is the throat (the thyroid gland), the sixth is the third eye (center of the forehead), and the seventh is the crown of the head.

Typically, in yoga philosophy also, the throat chakra is associated with the intellect, the heart with emotion, and the solar plexus with power. And, these are the three chakras loosely associated with the three centers spoken of in Fourth Way or Gurdjieffian work—the thinking center, the feeling center and the moving center. In Gurdjieff's work there are actually six centers spoken of, because each of the three mentioned above have both a lower and a higher aspect.

Orage, an eminent disciple of Gurdjieff, diagramed these six centers and associated them with the chakras as follows: 1 - lower moving center (first chakra), 2 - lower feeling center (third chakra), 3 - lower thinking center (fifth chakra), 4 - higher thinking center (sixth chakra), 5 - higher feeling center (fourth chakra), and the sixth and last center, the higher moving center (second chakra).

Orage said that the way one evolves is directly, linearly, from center to center (rather than from chakra to chakra). So, if one

---

1 This commentary is based on *The Gospel According to Orage,* from a chapter called "Activation of Centers." (Book is out of print.)

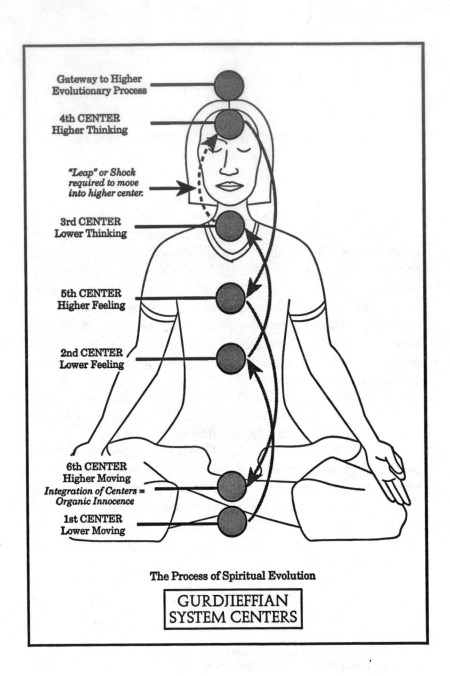

Gateway to Higher
Evolutionary Process

4th CENTER
Higher Thinking

"Leap" or Shock
required to move
into higher center.

3rd CENTER
Lower Thinking

5th CENTER
Higher Feeling

2nd CENTER
Lower Feeling

6th CENTER
Higher Moving

Integration of Centers =
Organic Innocence

1st CENTER
Lower Moving

The Process of Spiritual Evolution

GURDJIEFFIAN
SYSTEM CENTERS

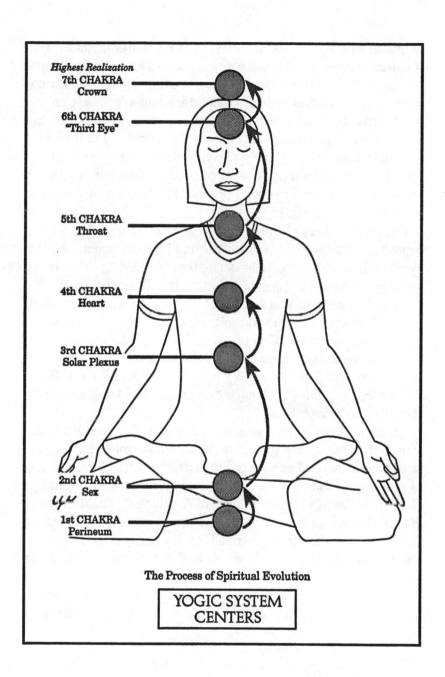

Highest Realization
7th CHAKRA
Crown

6th CHAKRA
"Third Eye"

5th CHAKRA
Throat

4th CHAKRA
Heart

3rd CHAKRA
Solar Plexus

2nd CHAKRA
Sex

1st CHAKRA
Perineum

The Process of Spiritual Evolution

YOGIC SYSTEM
CENTERS

wants to embody the Work, and if the first center is not awake, it doesn't matter what other centers are awake—you don't have the proper foundation. If you don't have the proper foundation, then no matter what kind of phenomena you are able to create arbitrarily, or accidentally, it essentially has no value for the Work. It's just phenomena. (In "New Age" circles you find a lot of people who are extremely psychic, clairvoyant—and totally weird. Some of them can't carry on a coherent conversation. A lot of yogis in India have wild phenomena too, but no coherent process in their lives.)

One of the ideas of the Gurdjieff work is to completely integrate your Being—to integrate all the centers. In terms of higher Work, this enables you to be consistent, and bring integrity to vows you make, among other things. It is literally impossible to be responsible in Work terms if your Being isn't integrated. You may make vows and commitments from an "I" that means it, and then another "I" pops up and you function completely mechanically. You break your vow and don't even have any choice about it. You are run by your lack of integration. Work ideas of responsibility and obligation are just academic principles if there's no integration.

In yoga philosophy, the whole idea is to function from the fourth chakra up, and to negate the bottom three chakras, particularly the second chakra or sex center—which in most yogas is seen as the chakra which gets you in trouble. It's the chakra that's associated with desire and all the "lower" considerations. But in this scheme, as Orage presents it, without integrating the second chakra in a mature way it's impossible to realize the full potential of the Work. Actually, the second chakra is the final key.

Let me start from this prospective in talking about centers. The first center is the basic moving center and is associated with the perineum, or the seat of *kundalini*[2] in the body. It is associated with shitting, and fear, and staying alive in purely instinctual terms. So, for example, in any moving art—like dance or martial arts—whoever brings instinct to it is going to be better at it.

The feeling center is associated with the solar plexus, not the heart. We tend to associate emotions with the heart. "I'm heartbroken... My heart aches... My heart swelled with joy..." We usually associate the heart with feeling, because of the language of our culture. Yet actually, it is all the false emotion or lower emotion associated with the heart that is "heart-breaking," because it makes the heart impotent. It bypasses the heart, cuts it off, avoids it. Lower feeling occurs in the solar plexus.

The thinking center is typically associated with the head because that's where our brain is, and we generally believe that thinking happens in the brain. Actually, the thyroid gland, or the fifth chakra, is the location of the lower thinking center. It is where ego resides at the primate level.

To activate the higher centers requires a shock. Moving from center one...to two... to three can happen energetically through very basic practices and through ordinary maturity, but you can't get from center three to four just by maturing ordinarily. To open up higher center functioning requires a shock.

Now the shock can be consciously given by the Teacher himself, the way Gurdjieff did, or through the Benediction[3] of a real Teacher, or the shock can happen accidentally. A bodily illness, the loss of a loved one, the birth of a child, or some emotional

---

2 kundalini - powerful energy that resides at the base of the spine. The kundalini can move up the spine into the other chakras or centers spontaneously, or more likely when specific practices (especially the use of breathing techniques) are applied.

3 Benediction - the personal Help which the spiritual guide or Master makes available through Divine Influence.

trauma...lots of things could produce the kind of explosive energy that is required. But first, before the explosive energy can be effective, the body needs to be in a state in which it is receptive to the energy exchange. If the body is in a state of too much tension and the explosion happens, it just shatters. Instead of transforming or alchemitizing, it just breaks. That's why it is so important to know what you're doing when intentionally providing shock, like Gurdjieff did. If you provide shock at the wrong time, then what happens is you break what it is you're providing shock to. You damage it, instead of giving it the necessary boost. In the same way, putting rocket fuel in the car would blow it up instead of making it go faster, because you need a special type of engine to burn rocket fuel.

• • •

To integrate the Work in your life, the first of the centers that needs to be established as the foundation platform, from which the other higher centers can naturally evolve without aberration, is the higher thinking center. We tend to look at the higher thinking center as something that's sort of "extra." It would be nice to have it, but we really want to get to higher feeling. The higher feeling center seems like the plum—having to do with poetry, real sentiment, compassion and all that. The higher feeling center is associated with the heart. But, actually, the higher feeling center is only the middle process within this evolutionary, transformational, alchemical development of higher centers.

The highest center is the higher moving center, which is associated with Organic Innocence. Within this center, you simply move in relationship to stimuli as empowered by, or under the power of, the Will of God. Everything is obvious. If the centers are developed in order (chakras 1, 3, 5, 6, 4, 2) and integrated, the final revelation is the maturity of the higher moving center—not the higher feeling center. The higher feeling center is developed along the way, out of the transformational process that is the blueprint of the human being.

Fourth Way terminology would say that the seventh center, which we haven't mentioned here yet, is where you begin to live with a soul. The seventh center is the gateway to the soul, but you don't get to that without this prior evolutionary process.

Typically, in yoga, the idea is to raise the *kundalini* linearly through the seven chakras until it opens the crown, the *sahasrar,* and you become and radiate light. However, if you push through the centers without going in the proper order, which happens by leaping chakras, you may not be able to come back to them. As the life force, or kundalini, moves through the chakras, *kriyas* (involuntary bodily movements) result from pushing through blocks. If you push through blocks in the wrong way, you rupture the chakras so that you can't go back to them when you need to.

The intensity of the phenomenon that occur at centers four, five and six, and the kind of drabness of phenomena down at centers one, two and three has been the motivating force behind so many widespread systems that use the yogic model as their base. This model typifies the search for experience, because experience at the higher levels is so mindblowing and experiences at the lower levels are just ordinary.

My experience (never having intentionally moved the energy to the degree that it was obvious it could be) has emphasized the need to allow the *shakti* or *kundalini* its own play so that the Context of Divine Influence, which is not the context of traditional yoga, defines everything that goes on in our lives.

If Divine Influence contextually defines how *shakti* moves, it will move by leaping chakras (as in the Orage diagram), not linearly (as in the traditional yoga diagram). If *kundalini* were triggered spontaneously and there were no control of it, it would tend, of its own, to move through these centers, but not to damage them at all. It would move through very easefully, very gracefully, without producing any damage. The key is that it not be manipulated. For instance, when devotion arises spontaneously it is an amazing phenomenon, but when it is forced it can produce phenomena that are actually damaging to the organism. People can throw themselves into devotional frenzies and end up damaging the possibility of real maturation in the feeling center.

Kundalini in the yogic model wants to move upward, chakra by chakra. Frequently, when you begin to pray earnestly, when you think you're meditating and doing spiritual work, what you will feel is tremendous sexual energy—sometimes overwhelming sexual desire. The biological energy wants the *kundalini* to move straight up; wants it to shatter through the second chakra or sex center. However, when it shatters through the second chakra, it leaves people sexless. People may move into higher centers and appear very light and very gentle and very soft, but also there is no passion. They're "dead"!

Getting from the lower thinking (fifth chakra) to the higher thinking (sixth chakra) is a whole different story. Again, you need shock to get there (to the sixth chakra). And, once there, you descend—you go back down to get to the higher feeling (fourth chakra) and higher moving (second chakra) centers.

● ● ●

Ideally, moving from center one to two to three should be the developmental process of a young human being, but we do not develop the centers in order. Rather our primate biology organically develops the chakras as in the yogic system, and therefore touches the centers out of order.

The first stage of life (from birth to age 7) is the moving stage. In the second stage of life (from 7 to 14) we develop emotionally. However, within our culture we are trained during this second stage to focus on discrimination and intellect. Instead, what should be trained from 7 to 14 years of age are all our relational qualities: hospitality, service, compassion, etc. Then, from 14 to 21 years of age the training should essentially focus on discrimination and a certain kind of analytical thinking—essentially what is taught in university philosophy classes.

Because adults are typically stuck somewhere down at the second chakra/sex center, children get to see and feel that sexual obsession from adults around them. They begin to develop or intensify their attention on that center very early in life.

Normally, children will just play with themselves very innocently. Girls will play with themselves because they find they can stick fingers in there, and boys will play with themselves because it sticks out. Infants will do that as a natural investigation of the body. When adults observe that behavior, and imply something in regards to it, the child feels it and gets stuck there because the child doesn't understand the adult's energy, fascination and confusion surrounding sexuality.

● ● ●

Usually, the first three centers fight with one another for control. The feeling center fights with the thinking center or the moving center. The first step in moving beyond this war is to activate the higher thinking, because that harmonizes the thinking center. When you activate the higher thinking center it combines with the lower thinking center; then the higher feeling combines with the lower feeling; and finally the higher moving combines with the lower moving. You end up still with three centers, but with no conflict, no war.

Activating higher thinking is like enlivening "the observer." For example, even when you're feeling helpless and out of control, you can still have a sense of yourself being helpless and out of control.

For the human organism to fulfill its evolutionary potential in the flesh requires the activation and maturation of the higher thinking, higher feeling and higher moving centers. The Baul practices of breath and the use of sexual energy are key in all of this. Without the higher consideration, or a tantric consideration of sexual energy and what that is, there can be no integration of the higher moving center. If there is no integration of the moving center, there is no completion of the organism as an alchemitized whole. The only way the higher moving center gets matured is through the use of sexual energy, because it's associated with the sexual chakra. There is no way of avoiding sexual energy (which doesn't mean sex, but does mean sexual energy). There is no way of avoiding sexual energy in considering the possibility of fulfilling the Work in a lifetime. It's impossible.

Now there are people who have used sexual energy without sex. I think we can believe the stories told about Nityananda's[4] work with his female devotees. He was using sexual energy without anything to do with sex. That's the hard way, of course. But then, maybe not. Maybe that's the easy way. One really has no grasp of what this final step means until one has arrived at this higher and lower thinking center integration and this higher and lower feeling center integration.

The higher moving center and the proper use of sexual energy are among the last things to work on—a very big thing to keep in mind for all of us aspiring tantrikas. There ain't no such thing as tantra without higher thinking and higher feeling. You get to tantric sexuality after compassion, not before compassion. You can force these issues, which is what a lot of the tantric practices do. But in the Tibetan Buddhist practices, you don't get any of the tantric sexual practices without having gone through the complete catalog of other practices that address all the other centers. It's never taken out of context. In the West, it's taken out of context, like raising kundalini can be taken out

---

4   Nityananda - a renowned twentieth-century Hindu saint and spiritual teacher.

of context. You do certain tantric exercises before integration, and what you do is you ruin the sex center from its possibilities. You stop the gears.

The higher feeling center is characterized by true emotion. And true emotion is not self-referencing. Now, everybody has sympathetic feelings. But there's a difference between sympathetic feelings and true emotion. True emotion is when you feel another's pain. Sympathetic emotion is when you feel for others. For example, somebody has some tragedy, and you're feeling it as if it had happened to you, which is self-referencing. "Geez, that must be awful," because if it happened to you then you would feel awful. You identify. In true emotion it *is* happening to you.

If one had matured in the higher feeling center but did not have discrimination, one couldn't walk out the door or pick up a newspaper without being devastated by emotionality. So, another reason you've got to have the higher thinking center functioning is because it involves discrimination. It gives you the ability to feel without being completely overwhelmed and debilitated by the feeling.

The sex center is also sometimes called the power center. When you develop the power center without higher thinking and higher feeling, essentially what you have is a maniac. Look at the most violently powerful people. They're all sexually frustrated.

Imagine what happens when people essentially misinterpret all of their emotions for higher feelings. For instance, in many spiritual groups you find men who assume that—because they have a certain emotional disposition by nature, and are always expressing feelings—they are developed in the higher feeling center, when they aren't at all. Since the next obvious form of development after the higher feeling center is the higher moving center, which is associated with sex, these men are going around being "tantric masters" with a lot of women.

All aberrant emotions are due to wrong thinking. So, the higher thinking center is the key—not only because it is the foundation of the higher centers, but also because it objectifys the illusions of the battle between "I's."

Higher thinking is having discrimination, and discrimination gives you an overview or a perspective of the Work. Once the higher thinking center is activated, you would never again forget to make use of Enquiry. It would spontaneously arise at times in which it was particularly useful. Enquiry is the obvious way to bring a perspective to the three lower centers.

Our primary work is to establish "majority vote" at the moving, thinking and feeling centers, and to activate the higher thinking center; and then to go on from there, while the lower three centers settle into their actual relationship to each other. When these three centers are able to fulfill their essential function without the interference of the others, that's majority vote. If you have a 51 percent vote, even though you can still have 49 percent interference, that 51 percent effectively prevents the interference of the other centers.

The longer one works in a School[5], the more one will have phenomena that are associated with the higher centers. (Even though all of these phenomena might show up for individuals who have never heard of spiritual work, one would not even begin a process of real Work until one became associated with a School, and a real Teacher.) The centers start to be touched in a certain way. Randomly, a student will experience the activation of the higher feeling center, but it doesn't mean that integration has taken place. The most important thing to realize is that integration is the maturation of the alchemical process-not just the opening of one of the centers, or the experiencing of one of the centers.

---

5 School - in this book, when capitalized, it refers to a group or community under the guidance of a spiritual teacher or Master.

The higher moving center is that which animates an organically innocent being. When that is animated, it doesn't mean you're perfectly healthy, it means when the Work requires something, you're there for it—your response is purely instinctual. Ordinarily when the Work needs us we aren't there for it because we've got lower center considerations. "What about this?" "What about that?" "What about family?" "What about health?" We've got a million considerations. "What about diet?" "Do I need vitamins?" That's why we need *Draw No Conclusions Mind*. If we function from the position of *Draw No Conclusions Mind* it doesn't mean we won't have serious sorrow in our lives, but we will leap first and ask questions later. Sometimes the questions are going to make us very upset. They are going to make our lives miserable. But the point is, a miserable life aligned with the Work is simply Real, and a life unaligned with the Work, because you're always considering the cost of action, is not.

Either you are dead or you are Alive. If you are Alive, the Work defines your life no matter how much pain it causes. If you are dead, you weigh the pain.

● ● ●

Meditation works with feeling, study works with thinking, and exercise deals with moving. That's a very loose definition of the relationship between the spiritual practices of this School and the centers. As for the practice of breathing, initially it has to do with just breathing deeply, like a baby breathes, free of constriction. Breath relates to the feeling center. When you are emotional, people say, "Take a deep breath." What happens immediately when you take a deep breath? "Feelings" that are not feelings go away. If you breathe deeply, you can only feel what's real. You can't feel what isn't real feeling. Once the higher thinking center is activated, breath becomes a way of opening the heart, and exercise becomes a way of bringing energy flow to a point at which the use of sexual energy can be transformative—the final alchemical mordant[6] necessary for integration of the centers.

So all the spiritual practices recommended to students in this School have their basic components and then their higher components. For instance, when you intentionally practice Tai Chi or any form of martial arts, you get to a point when you begin to feel the energy "moving you," over and against "you moving the energy." In the same way, the key to effective transformation of sexual energy is letting the energy move you instead of you moving the energy.

Even if all your centers are integrated, you have to build the energy to a certain point to be able to specifically activate the right use of sexuality. Once you are functioning from the position of Organic Innocence, you just function that way contextually. Even so, it doesn't mean that every time you have sex, it's cosmic. You still have to apply certain mechanics to get to the point where sex itself is "doing something." The lower centers must be warmed up. You don't just jump into the higher feeling center immediately. You don't walk in the room, see your mate, and all of a sudden you're overwhelmed with higher emotion. You've got to warm up. How you warm up is through ordinary, basic, life-level behavior. You sit down and say, "Hi, honey, how are you doing? Did you have a nice day? What's for dinner? Oh, great. I love that." You've got to build a certain momentum. The fastest way to kill momentum is to come in, look at your mate, get this negative look on your face and say, "Did you get your hair cut today?" Right away you've got a furious war of "I's": the woman wants to say, "Yes, dear," and not react, but another "I" is saying "That stupid bastard. He never compliments me.

---

6   mordant - a substance used in dyeing to fix the coloring matter. Applied in terms of alchemy, here, the mordant is the substance or force or influence that allows any transformational process to take hold.

Jesus! He hasn't given me a compliment in years. What an asshole." While the moving center is saying, "You haven't seen him all day. Go and give him a hug. Say hello and invite him to sit down." So you've got this tremendous conflict. And the thinking center right away pulls out all the psychology: "That's the way he is. He is a little boy now..." You've got a war of centers.

You warm up the coils by not creating a war of centers. You warm them up by keeping the lower centers integrated—just being an ordinary, relational, human being.

Secret 49: Tantra—A Dangerous Path

The traditional practice of tantra essentially means meeting and going through the elements of the underworld[7] converting these elements rather than attempting to escape them or ignore them, as a way to realization. We need fear, desires, illnesses, greed, possessiveness and all of the life-negative qualities that each of us has to some degree, and through working with them we transform them. Even if we didn't need them, they are an integral part of us, and must be recognized. But we *do* need them. They help make up who we are in the upperworld. Without them, we would not be human and therefore would not have the Divine Possibility and Divine opportunity that human existence is. Through working *with* these forces, not in spite of them, they are transformed. That's essentially what tantra is.

Different tantric schools use different elements in their practice—sex, alcohol, tobacco or other things. Yet they are all the same in their focus on the transformation of substances—i.e. alchemy, in the true sense of the word.

The ascent alone—the melting into light as attempt to avoid going through the underworld—is not the way of tantra. In tantric work one can't relax. The tantrika has got to keep his or her eyes open and pay attention. Alertness must be constant because the dangers are many.

---

7 underworld - In the shamanistic worldview, the underworld is the domain of demons, the residence of life-negative forces, pain, suffering, the darkness. The underworld, however, must be passed through to gain entry to the upperworld, the domain of the gods and spirits.

In tantra you essentially work with the nuclear power of sex. This is not something you play around with. You know...a hot woman comes along and you look at her and think, "Ah, she'd be good." So you ask, "Want to be a consort?" You don't play around with these things because they are not only uniquely transformative, they are also significantly dangerous. One can be made immortal or one can be destroyed. If, however, you can trust your teacher or source of help, you don't need to worry that all hell will break loose. But still, I'm personally very careful in this domain, and conservative to the ninth degree.

Many scholars and students of tantric practice say that one should never enter any kind of tantric work without a Teacher. The implied reasons are that a Teacher will observe the practice, recognize the signs of maturity and the signs of illusion, and act as a feedback mechanism. It is assumed, of course, that the teacher is capable of such wisdom through his or her own experience and Revelation. There is also the unspoken element that when there is an honest, devotional relationship between the student and the Teacher, the Teacher can provide the necessary mordant for the student's transformational practice. Without that catalyzing ingredient, one doesn't really transform. Rather, substances stay constant (unchanged) but just shift around. This role of the teacher, however, is not spoken of because the path is so dangerous and one must not get the idea that he or she can rest and just float on the Teacher's influence or be carried on the Teacher's back. One has got to keep one's eyes open and pay attention.

It is said that entering the path of tantra is more dangerous than taming and riding a tiger—more dangerous than many things one would never do if one had any sense. It is essential to remember what this work is about so that we don't get lackadaisical or begin to take it for granted. One must pay attention even in the midst of intense excitement, euphoria, distraction and fascination, and must not get seduced into sleep or unconsciousness. The help and Influence of an impeccable Teacher or guide is crucial.

• • •

You need to understand that the sexual center is the focal point in the body for transformation. Therefore, if you are being alchemitized, you will tend to have a very hot sexual center, and you need to know the difference between a hot sexual center and lust. They are not the same.

If sexual energy is channelled into communion, the body becomes bright, luminous, attractive. The aura becomes alive and tempting. The voice becomes smooth and charismatic.

In this condition you must know who you are... or honey...you is in big trouble!

Secret 50: Sex: Its Transcendent Possibilities

There are many techniques in conventional tantra. In one book I read, the author recommends that for one month the partners are not supposed to touch. So they start out, the first week, sitting across the room from one another, clothed, and they just look at each other (ya know, the old misty-eyed romantic bit). The second week they sit directly in front of one another, clothed, and they look in their partner's eyes for an hour (probably hiding lust behind "the gaze" of course). The third week they take their clothes off and sit and look again. And the fourth week they sit without clothes on, and with knees touching, looking into one another's eyes for an hour (being very careful not to peek at tits, pricks, or body hair). Then one is supposed to be primed for real tantra. Can you imagine that these books actually tell you to do that?

Well, by the time four weeks is up people jump on one another like they're mad, and what takes place then is eighty percent fantasy and twenty percent physical. Of course they have a great time! Who wouldn't after a month of percolating repressed passion. Of course the experience is going to be overwhelmingly powerful. But it's fantasy. It's not tantra.

Another approach some authors take to "tantra" is to show you all these amazing positions—upside down, backwards, from the front, from the back, with fingers, toes or noses...Here again, real tantra doesn't have anything to do with what position you're in. It makes no difference at all.

● ● ●

Typically, when men make love, their whole body is a knot of tension. Their abdomen is tensed and their shoulders are up and their jaws are clenched and they're gripping something—the woman, the bed, the air. They're wired. There isn't a gentle relaxation, a joy in the beauty of sexual communion.

Several years ago, in a book called *ESO, Extended Sexual Orgasm*...or something like that...many techniques were given. There are technical ways of reaching a state in which there is a certain pleasurable sensation that is so intense that orgasm itself will be recognizable, but barely. Nonetheless, there is a highly significant difference between that physical state when it is achieved through mechanical means, and the relaxation into the possibilities of true intimacy and communion.

When that book first came out people were saying, "Oh, since I've read this book, my life has never been the same!" But pretty quickly people with any sensitivity realized they were still suffering just as much. Life was not clearer or more integral because of 20-minute orgasmic peaks. At random times when they had sex they momentarily forgot about their suffering, but at other times they were the same people. No change. No transformation was either evident or true of them. They were simply able to technically manipulate the body to achieve that physiological state.

If, on the other hand, one moves into that state as a spontaneous form of communion, a very different possibility is present. In fact, it would be highly unlikely that someone in this situation would ever be the same person again. Suffering may not dissolve so completely that the next morning there would never be a single worry about any kind of burden again. But, if one had moved into that space of heightened nerve sensitivity as a spontaneous result of the intensity of their *sadhana* within their relationship, a definite difference would be made.

What we are describing here is a spontaneous experience of essence[8] versus training the machine[9] to produce a certain effect.

• • •

With the usual genital, stress-release orgasm, the nervous system goes down the drain. Everything goes out with orgasm, not just sperm. (The psychological association made with ejaculation is tremendous.) Life, energy, *shakti*, attention—everything goes out. Ejaculation is essentially neither here nor there; it isn't the point, attention is the point. But, man explodes and everything is lost. If it were just ejaculation and there was a different mood in the man's body, so much more would be possible. Such greater sensations would be present.

The physical practice of tantra by men involves the utilization, but not necessarily the strict preservation, of semen, in conjunction with the proper disposition of sexual energy and *intention*. The subtle practice of tantra involves the right use of *attention*. The same principle applies to women, of course. Women have a sexual fluid that's not just the lubricating fluid that arises during sex. There is actually a seminal fluid which doesn't contain sperm, but contains other similar chemistries as in a man. So this consideration applies to everybody—man, woman...or sacred cow. (Since Ramana Maharshi said that animals get enlightened, too, we have to apply the practice of true tantra to cows—although it's not likely that bulls will control ejaculation. But perhaps cows could get some help from this discussion.)

When sexual activity is somewhat regular, a lot of semen is produced in the man, and a lot of sexual fluid in the woman.

---

8   essence - intrinsic nature; typically referring to the fundamental qualities of a person, as contrasted to what is conditioned and learned by ego.

9   the machine - the "human biological machine"; the program-driven, unawakened aspect of consciousness.

When this fluid is allowed to be reabsorbed into the body, rather than expelled or expressed, the chemistry involved in that fluid is sympathetic to certain hormonal secretions by areas of the brain—like the pineal gland, which is traditionally associated with the "third eye." We don't know all that these glands can do, but we do have a high degree of circumstantial evidence that stimulation of these glands can produce mystical vision, revelation, higher creativity, and so on. The utilization of sex is one way of activating the higher glands.

Since ancient times, it has been known that the sexual act is literally a generator, and a catalyst. Many spiritual Masters and adepts have used sex as a method to encourage communion with higher levels of consciousness. It wasn't that they used women as objects or that women Masters used men as objects. Rather, male Masters used the communication of sex with women in worship. Sex wasn't to them simply a matter of keeping the old lady happy. It was a matter of using the incredible power available within sex to generate higher conscious experience. In a sense, they were evolving the human race through the use of sex. It's very common to see pictures from ancient China, and from the Hindu and the Buddhist traditions showing the gods with their consorts. In the Orient, beautiful artwork was designed to celebrate sexual union in its transcendent capacity. People weren't embarrassed about it. It was quite ordinary because work on higher levels was accepted and recognized.

Real tantra is not a matter of looking in one another's eyes and building up desire to the point of madness. If you understand real tantra, you can hop on and screw like a bandit and it doesn't make a bit of difference. The communication in real tantra has to do with the understanding of the woman's energy and the man's energy. It doesn't have to do with some "lovey-dovey, feely-touchy, let's-get-our-minds-together-and-think-as-one" idea. It has nothing to do with that. Fantasies of oneness arise out of that kind of tantric practice, but that's not true tantra. True tantra is founded in the already present understanding that you are not separate to begin with. It's not a matter of trying to generate a telepathic feeling of oneness. That happens, certainly, but so what? What does that mean? You are just as messed up the rest of the day when you're not doing your tantric practice. True tantra has to do with a crystal clear understanding of man, woman, and alchemy.

Women might be described as basically being receptive, and men as basically being aggressive. Listen carefully to this...it is a secret esoteric mystery: Since women symbolize Shakti, the goddess, form, activity, movement, energy, and men symbolize Shiva, who is the formless Absolute, who is simply consciousness—the union of Shiva/Shakti involves ascent by the woman and descent by the man. When Shiva and Shakti *become* one another, that's what is called perfect union. Then the sexes disappear and there is only what is arising in the field of Reality. You have that process typified in the symbolic and archetypal relationship of physical man to physical woman. Woman ascends, Shakti to Shiva, and man descends, Shiva to Shakti. Man becomes form, and woman becomes formless. The cycle of activity that sexual tantra involves is descent by the man and ascent by the woman. Orgasm can happen, but nonlocalized nonejaculatory orgasm by the man keeps his energy connected to the woman and doesn't rip him away from her.

Tantra, when properly engaged, can be the catalyst to great creativity for ordinarily mundane minds. It's not that any of us that haven't become geniuses aren't inherently geniuses. It's simply that on one level our body chemistry has not allowed us to open up certain channels of expression and creativity. Tantra can do that, through the vitalization of certain higher glands that are not vitalized in other ways.

I recently read a book of love letters written by the composer, Chopin, who was a creative genius in the realm of art, and probably could have been a saint if he had chosen to. In these letters he expressed his passion to his lover, how he just wanted to come to her and screw the hell out of her. But, he said, "When I'm with you and we're screwing all the time, I can't write...not even a line of music. And being away from you here..." (he was on vacation) "...I've been writing like a champ." (I'm modernizing his language.) Then he ends the letter, "Oh, the hell with music. I'm coming back. So what if I can't write. What's an etude compared to..." He called her vagina Dflat major, because the note Dflat on the piano is a black key with a white key on either side. They had this little code, you know, and when they went to visit his dad, he'd say to her, "Oh, how's your Dflat major?" She'd sing a little note, and they'd wink at one another, and the folks would wonder what was going on.

• • •

Transcendental sex doesn't look alike for all men, or women. For some women, nonorgasmic sex is absolutely transcendental only if the circumstances are appropriate and Love is present. For other women, transcendental sex is something that comes at the end of a whole string of orgasms and higher and higher peaks. Conservation of orgasm is the context, but the content (the many forms) can be infinite in variety and texture.

Sex can bring people to the edge of manifestation, to the edge of creation. Usually, the only time a man gets vaguely close to that is when conception takes place in intercourse and the man knows it. That can push a man into the realization of sex as a transcendental experience. It usually doesn't, but it can if it happens quickly enough. It can happen if the man doesn't stop the realization accompanying conception before it moves onto its logical conclusion, which is not just that, "Me and the little woman have created new life far out." It can lead to an impersonal, transcendental realization about creation itself, not about the creation of a baby. But that's where it usually ends. Men get "blown out" because of the communion that takes place when that's realized, but they don't let it go on. That's not done on purpose, of course. It's pretty dramatic for Ego to feel it has duplicated itself. But creation is not about Ego, it's about feeding the Divine. If a man realizes that, he has found something. He will live that principle all the time.

• • •

A real relationship is an experiment in alchemy. An intimate relationship, sooner or later, becomes a very intense experiment because you alchemitize one another if you are really together in a bonded way. To alchemitize means to biologically and organically transform the being (encompassing both gross and subtle domains). Actually, that's only the first stage. The more mature stages of it have to do with transmuting substances. In a relationship, people transmute one another. They literally alter the structure of one another's beings.

Of course, both people in a couple are not going to move "over the line" of transformation together. That is guaranteed. People all change at different rates, in different forms. Whoever moves "over the line" of transformation first is never going to say "I love you" and have it mean what it meant before...ever. It's impossible. One who moves over the line has a new vision of reality—a broader perspective if you will. So, you have to be prepared to hear "I love you" and have it mean something beyond what you can recognize at the time, but feel the truth and beauty of it and rest in that. Romanticism is extraordinary, valuable and wonderful in its domain, but the domain of "I love you" in the ultimate meaning of what love is, is not the domain of romanticism.

• • •

Gurdjieff talked about creating a soul. He said that until you create a soul for yourself the Work is of no use to you, or at least is of no more use than a temporary bandaid—something that is eliminated when the body passes away.

Being in a sexual relationship is, for each individual, like a direct and viable opportunity for creating a soul. This is why you shouldn't just fuck anyone off the streets. If you fuck anyone, you're petitioning God to begin to create a soul, with this other person as the necessary chemical ingredient needed to continue this building process.

Imagine the havoc you wreak if you're involved in lots of fast-and-flashy love affairs, and you've got loose "soul" ends all over the place—karmic connections that create a madhouse of unravelling requirements (or even more imposing, of "ravelling" requirements).

You aren't getting on God's good side here! Every time God gets the message to create a soul, he (I'm talking about God as being a man, since he's usually referred to as "He" anyway. It's just a convention so don't get all riled up...) gets a kind of hard-on, like this Divine Erection so to speak. And you all know how uncomfortable unfulfilled passion feels. If you're with a cock-teaser or a cunt-teaser, you know how frustrating and maddening it can be. (A cunt-teaser is rare, of course—men being as weak and spineless as they are, and having no integrity. Usually when a man flirts he means it. He wants his 30-second "dip" and his orgasm.)

At any rate, if someone toys around with your affections, you aren't real keen on offering them the goodies over and over. God is like that too. When there's a true union, it's like you are creating something. To create that is to create it "unto all eternity." Every time you slip your thing into her thing, or let him slip *his* into *yours,* you're signaling the Divine. I'm talking about you, not just any human being. Some human beings are just animals and this doesn't apply to animals. Most of you are conscious enough so that when you dip the "old wick" or have the "old wick" dipped, you begin something substantial. You send a signal out into the universe. If you have no integrity about that, God gets pretty annoyed and, after awhile, instead of responding, it becomes like the boy who cried wolf. God hears the signal and looks and says, "Oh, it's just him (or her) again." Then, even when you want to be serious, he doesn't take you seriously—which is why it's difficult for some people who come to spiritual life to form a serious relationship. God doesn't listen to them anymore. They try and they try, and nothing happens. They say, "Gosh, I'm with the spiritual Master. Why isn't my relationship blossoming?" It's because of your past history. No soul, no peace, no satisfaction.

• • •

Any practice of higher esoteric techniques should only be utilized actively when the basic stuff has been dealt with. If one's personality is overwhelmingly negative, depressive or pessimistic, sexual tantra shouldn't be used. Sexual tantra is not a healing force. It isn't designed to clean the cesspool. If one's basic relationships are optimistic and celebratory, if one celebrates God in the company of other devotees, then one is ready to begin to study and investigate the practice of tantra. If one's relationships are always about protecting territory, or about envy, fear, or aggressiveness, then to even consider practicing sexual tantra is absurd because what it will do is irritate whatever tendencies one has. It will magnify them a hundred times— you will become very creative in negative, destructive and masochistic forms. But likewise, if your relationships are full and celebratory, and you "love God," the practice of sexual tantra will magnify that, will "irritate" that, in a sense. It will unleash energies, clarity, insight and revelation that will not get unleashed in other ways.

Irritation is irritation—it can be positive or negative. An irritation can create a pearl in an oyster, or create destruction. Either one can and will happen.

Secret 51: It's All The Same

There's a secret teaching (about both sexuality and spirituality) that is at the essence of this Work...and then there's a public teaching. Listen to this—the secret teaching is: You can have a "needle dick" or a "sausage dick," but no matter what a dick looks like, when you plug it into the socket and you "rev up" the energy, it achieves the same results.

The point is that the body is the real dick and the appendage is just the plug on the end of the circuitry. The nervous system is the ultimate dick, and the nervous system is the same in every human being—man or woman. It doesn't matter what the dick looks like outside. I had a great shock when I was a waterboy for the football team in high school. (They used to call us "managers," but what we did was run out on the field during the timeouts and give the guys on the football team a sponge to suck on, and then rake the mud out of their cleats so they could run better.) It was a great shock to me when I realized, in observing the shower ritual after the game, that these six-foot-five-inch, 240-pound linemen had dicks no bigger than mine. It was profound. I mean, I almost woke up then.

We have a saying in English, "Don't judge a book by its cover." It doesn't matter what the dick looks like, because when you connect to the proper circuitry, it effects exactly the same results. No man who plugs into the proper circuitry will feel any different than any other man plugged into the same circuitry. No woman who plugs into the appropriate circuitry will feel any different than any other woman.

Of course there are various idiosyncrasies in individual relationships with different people. But, if you experience what I am talking about there comes a point when you're plugged into the right circuitry when it all becomes the same—when all the idiosyncrasies disappear, and woman becomes Woman, or man becomes Man. Every woman does not look the same on the surface, but is the same at the level of the Essential Feminine. That's the biggest secret of spiritual life. Have you effectively paid attention to that? That's all you have to know. It's all the same and I hope by now it's obvious I'm not talking about the circuitry of "pussy" and "prick" energetics.

The public teaching about spiritual work is that there are many levels of practice and maturity, and that one needs to have a certain amount of discipline and do a certain amount of formal practices, and pay attention to all of the protocol, and rise through the ranks...That no one gets to be in the "inner circle" without nine or ten years of work, and all that kind of stuff. But actually, all one needs is a map to the circuitry and they are set. There's nothing to it. It is the same for men and women because there is only God at the level of context and Realization. Only God.

How does the shift of Context, where one realizes there is only God, become permanent, rather than having a moment of freedom and then going back?

One must stop being a sexist pig, a misogynist, a feminist man-hater, a liberated woman, a "real man," and all of that. The definitions of all of these are effective obstacles to a permanent shift of context. You must be a human being before you are a man or a woman. You must be a Lover before you are a sex object. You must know joy before passion (or lust), generosity before greed, gentleness and compassion before superstition and prejudice. One must relax one's subjective view of reality, and come to rest in an attitude of *Draw No Conclusions Mind.* Allow the revelatory truth a chance to take seed, root, and sprout. Then you must feed the vision with action.

It's not good enough to speak eloquent words in public and beat your wife and children in private. You must, in essence, practice the Word, not just mouth it.

Nothing to it, eh?

Secret 52: The Difficulty of Tantric Vows

Most people's projection about tantric vows, if you want to take them down to their simplest interpretation, is: "Eat when you're hungry, fuck when you're horny and sleep when you're tired." This seems like a great way to live—very spontaneous, very self-fulfilling. It all seems so exciting and fresh, so natural.

However, in actual fact, the tantric vows are the most difficult to keep because they are the ones that have the most qualification—not objective qualification, but internal qualification. "Eat when you're hungry, fuck when you're horny and sleep when you're tired" is the most difficult thing to do because those vows mean doing these things free of any attachment or complication of ego. A nun's vows and a monk's vows are actually the easiest to keep because they are laid out to the letter and ego has nothing to do with them. Ego is not involved in discriminating in monastic vows. Certainly ego has its resistances, its struggles, its recoil, but the definitions and limits are exact and clear. All one needs to do is have discipline and will.

But to keep the tantric vows, one needs infinitely more than discipline. A practitioner could have all the discipline in the world and if he or she doesn't have discrimination, among other things, it wouldn't do a damn bit of good. And the discrimination required is startlingly clear and profoundly deep discrimination, not just a little bit of surface discrimination. One needs to be able to feel the most delicate subtleties and sense all the implications of every move. In tantric practice one doesn't make gold out of lead, as in traditional alchemy. Instead, one finds the proverbial needle in a haystack. Actually, it's more like finding a mustard seed in a massive pile of shit. Of course, this process is alchemical in the highest sense, but definitely not in the high-school chemistry class experimental sense.

Discrimination is about the difference between instinctual movement—essential movement—and ego movement. It is about spontaneity based on Divine Influence or the Will of God, arising in response to the immediate and objective needs of the moment or to the Absolute circumstantial reality. This type of spontaneity is not based on the usual manifestations of a man or woman (particularly strong in regards to eating, sexing, and sleeping), which are not really spontaneous at all. These usual manifestations are simply automatic and chronically habitual fulfillments of the strategy ego has designed, quite early in infancy or childhood, to assure the continuation of the survival of the Being as ego identifies it, or to avoid extinction as ego sees extinction.

The most essential characteristic of sexual practice, however, is not to clench up over it, not to stress out. Go along easefully and make your relationship work with attention and care. Give one another "food," and consider these ideas.

Secret 53: When It Hits

When Real tantra hits, it hits. Before it hits, it doesn't hit. I enjoy studying, so I've compiled a fairly broad body of information, but when something has hit me experientially that was not previously part of my experience, even when what I have studied has been perfectly clear and obvious, the realization has simply been that now the body knows what the head already knew. All of the so-called tantric ritual in the world isn't going to mean anything until Revelation hits. When it hits it hits; and until it hits, it doesn't hit. It's like your turn in the lottery. Life is a big crap shoot, and everybody hits their run sooner or later.

It's not something you can do anything about in order to increase your odds. You can't increase your odds but you can practice. How many times you have sex, or with whom, or how, is not going to increase the odds. When tantra hits, it hits. Life is like that. Our training is all to optimize our ability to use Revelation when it hits, not to make it happen faster—because we simply cannot.

Secret 54: Sexual Tantra:
Some Common Misconceptions

The greatest handicap to tantric sexuality is the fear of failure. "What if I breathe through the wrong nostril? What if I do the wrong mudra, imagine the wrong yantra, say the wrong mantra?" The biggest obstacle to tantric sexuality is feeling that you've got to do it right, or do it a certain way every time. Relax! For twenty-five years you screwed every which way, and nothing went wrong, did it? Now, all of a sudden, you get a little technique for breathing and you're worried. Listen, nothing is going to go wrong if you have an orgasm when you're not supposed to, or if you don't have an orgasm when you're supposed to, or if you breathe through the wrong nostril.

If we had thousands of years of cultural refinement that we were genetically heir to, and our systems could be balanced in line with our genetic disposition easily, we would have to be a little more careful. But we are gross, crude beings. Some yogic books say that if you breathe through the wrong channel at the wrong time, you can whack your nervous system out. But most of us are very gross beings and we don't have to worry about that.

At the same time, most of us could experience a Japanese tea ceremony and be knocked out, made speechless by the elegance of it. We do have a certain inclination for elegance, fortunately, even though we're pretty gross beings. After some years, perhaps you become a bit more sensitive because sadhana in a Real School naturally defines your nervous system in a much cleaner and purer way, and you begin to be responsive to more subtle things.

Don't worry about trying to develop sexual tantra. You can get so wrapped up in the lighting, the incense, and the music, that you become more tense than when you were a kid in 7th grade asking a girl to dance. Consider and work with the ideas, but don't get all tensed up about them.

● ● ●

Another of the big handicaps to tantric sex is vanity.

When you're ready to enter genuine sexual communion (genuine tantra), you're going to blow a few fuses and you're going to have to be a different human being afterwards. Imagine this, however—You're right there, at the edge, and what comes to mind? Vanity! "I'm sweating too much. What if somebody were watching? How's my hair? Am I doing it right?" Vanity. When a sexual encounter starts to escalate to a point where personality is losing its grip and essence is taking over, mind will come in and try to undermine your intention. Why? Because mind doesn't want the being to be changed.

● ● ●

Many women have a sexual drive that is defined by the urge to procreate. But this instinctual drive has been turned into an epidemic by confused, insecure, unconscious women. Madison Avenue has convinced all of us—men and women—that we should be interested in making love all the time, that it is a natural urge to couple endlessly without a break. To the false emotions this feels like a genuine urge, but it's purely a conditioned urge to sex twisted out of instinct.

Sexual communion confounds the urge to procreate. More accurately, it simply doesn't take it into consideration, because sexual communion is entirely free of the urge to orgasm—although orgasm may occur spontaneously. Conversely, sexual communion is not adverse to procreating either. It just isn't confused by moral or self-referenced issues. The urge to orgasm doesn't exist where sexual communion exists, but in the pure sense the urge not to have orgasm does not arise either.

• • •

Fear of Flying by Erica Jong, was a novel about a woman who was married to an Oriental psychiatrist. Where could you go for better sex? The Oriental part of him had perfect discipline and could screw her to the limit every time, and the psychiatrist part knew how to be the perfect partner. Yet, after a while, it got to be a drag. After a while, all she wanted him to do was have premature ejaculation—anything to be different. Perfect sex all the time isn't perfect sex. It's boring. Anything all the time, even sexual communion, even ecstasy, is a drag.

When you are in a relationship in which the matrix is sexual communion, still, once in a while you just screw. You know… you're on the plane going to Philadelphia with your partner… and you look at one another …and the lavatories are empty…so you go back there and practically push the damn walls down screwing each other. You aren't in sexual communion. You're just humping like animals and it's fine, spontaneous, pure. That's enough for a while, and it is wonderful and makes you ecstatic.

And next time you're together, you're in sexual communion.

• • •

The consideration of tantra is not about learning how to breathe properly so you can go home, work at it, and next week be able to tell Rajneesh or Sondra Ray a thing or two. Tantra is about deep, profound understanding, about manifesting a principle. If you practice diligently and sensitively, which I would recommend, the fruit of that practice may appear in months, or years, maybe not for ten years. But, incidentally, there will be the opportunity to realize what sexual communion is.

Sexual communion itself isn't the fruit of practice. What I'm suggesting is that when you see the opportunity of sexual communion—what it really means—all of your images of sex will be shattered. It might be years, having glimpsed the opportunity, before you can begin to put your body consistently behind the practice that will afford you that communion forever, every time you're together, physically or otherwise.

"High sex" doesn't have anything to do with communion. Communion is something else. There is "cosmic sex" so high that you can just lie back, half off the bed, without even the strength to open your eyes and your room will look like an opium den. That's different than communion.

So, once you glimpse the opportunity of sexual communion, it could be years before you could put your body in line with a practice that will afford you the ability to be in communion all the time, because it will shatter all of your sexual beliefs and expectations, all your chronic patterns and habits about sex.

Secret 55: Tantra and Objective Knowledge

Mind, even more than the heart, is the single most dynamic and comprehensive mechanism of manipulation and control in the entire body. The mind can stop the heart very easily if it's got enough reason to. Objective knowledge—knowledge that is exactly the same for everyone, man or woman, regardless of culture, age, race or religion—can only be recognized by a part of us that is not influenced, controlled by, or at the effect of mind. So it stands to reason that if the aim for any given human being is the realization of this objective knowledge, which is the same thing as the ultimate degree of self-development, or we could say Realization, then sooner or later one would have to come to look for a way of practicing that either transcends or works through the mind, a way that deals with it exactly the way it *is,* without being controlled or manipulated or at the effect of it. We would have to develop a sensing, data-gathering and informing mechanism that is not mind-sourced or mind-motivated.

The form or matrix that we animate as living beings, human beings, is not limited by what our eyes see to be the definition of our bodies. Our organic bodies actually inhabit many different dimensions. Objective knowledge, therefore, is communicated through organic levels of communication, but not through levels of communication that we are used to perceiving tangibly, or trained conventionally to rely on. Objective knowledge is communicated through an organic channel that is completely integral between people, but subtle rather than gross. We could say that such knowledge—That which is Objective—is communicated through a "field" rather than through a narrow channel or through a "line." For example, when a whole room of people is experiencing a certain kind of communication in which nothing need be said, and everybody understands exactly what's going on, this common knowledge that everyone perceives conjunctly is one form of such communication. There's an automatic agreement that's called "communion." That type of tacit understanding of one another's state of being is not a process of mind. It is literally impossible for mind to be in communion, except in the most superficial way, like in a state of psychic sympathy or empathy. In order for communion to take place, there must be a literal integration of elements of the subtle, organic domains of all of those in the bond or matrix of communion. If it's two people, there must be a literal organic integration; if there's a dozen people, there must be a literal organic integration. It's not just a mingling of auras. It's very different—a more comprehensive and blended process. It's like each individual loses his distinction as an "other," yet maintains the gross physical separation (obviously).

First of all, I think I need to put a warning in here. Some products include a warning, like those on cigarette packages in America: "Cigarette smoking may be dangerous to your health." In tantric yoga, this kind of information would be like the initiation after years of intense sadhana, and so I am hereby formally absolving myself of any problems that any of you may have by trying to implement this information in your lives without the help of a Teacher who knows what he or she is doing—which doesn't necessarily have to be me. (In fact, I hope it's not.) This information is very dangerous. Actually, to be bluntly honest, the reason I'm giving the information at all is because there are some students for whom this information is useful. The rest of you are the necessary grease for the wheel, as they say. I thought I needed to be bluntly honest, for an uncharacteristic change of pace.

Any single sexual event or experience is usually only satisfying for a short period of time, and not for weeks or months. However, given the data we are considering here, we should understand that one sexual encounter could be literally satisfying for weeks, unendingly. One event could satiate the feeding body for a great length of time. I don't mean you have to stay joined at the genitals for weeks. Really, a very short "union" could be satisfying for quite a long time, but the reason it usually isn't is because there's no organic communication, no blending, no subtle-body reciprocity. Even though two pieces of flesh are fairly intimately connected, that does not mean there's organic communication. When there is communion in sex, one session of lovemaking can last in intensity, fullness and pleasure, for weeks and even months.

An obvious question is, "Can there be organic integration if only one person is in communion with the Essential Being of the other even when the other is completely 'out of it?'" Yes, there can be. "If a sexual event were fully satisfying, would or could one still feel desire and enter into sexual communion again anyway?" Yes, of course. Why not? It is possible for one to be in communion with a piece of music by Bach, or with a painting, or with a statue by Rodin, so this consideration does not apply only to human beings. (I've never seen communion happen with a dog although some of you who have dogs for pets—with names like George, Myrtle, Betty, Paul or Austin Carter III—might think you have.)

In order for objective alchemy to be effected, there needs to be an organic integration between all of the levels involved in the two or more elements of the communion chamber. There needs to be a "blending of substances." This needs to be a real blending, not just a mix of sexual fluids, and blood, sweat and tears.

There are ways to develop the ability to relax in such a fashion that your organic being can integrate with another's organic being. This process is not a matter of doing anything aggressively, muscularly, intrusively. It is not a matter of becoming something you are not already. It's a matter of relaxing the obstacles that usually keep this process from happening; and mind is the primary creator of obstacles that effectively keep communion from happening.

Let's call that which is not under the control of mind, that which is not manipulated by mind, "objective consciousness," and that which is mind, "subjective consciousness." The difference between objective and subjective is that, in any given moment, to objective consciousness there's only one appropriate response to any given stimuli. Objective consciousness has no options for expression in any moment at all, no doubts, no confusion. It has no options, no alternatives. Subjective consciousness holds the possibility of many alternatives in every moment. To subjective consciousness there is always a choice...many choices to be made based on a critical or analytical consideration of observable and arbitrary data like emotional confusion and/or what one had for lunch today.

One minor qualification is that people's basic natures are different. The issue of mind has to do with the orientation towards who one is psychologically, not with who one is in truth. Some people are very gregarious, very outgoing. Some people are very quiet and reserved. Some people are highly emotional and some are cool and unemotional. Those things don't necessarily have anything to do with mind. They may, but not necessarily. If everyone reading this were to realize that which is prior to mind, or to realize objective consciousness, we would still show up very differently in our actions, moods, and preferences. Some of us would be very expressive and some of us would not be expressive. Mind does create particular postures and particular gestures, but also there are very basic differences in people. There are essential types of human beings, and those exist and remain regardless of whether mind is dominating or whether mind is being used as a tool by objective consciosuness. If you study the lives of Jesus, Buddha, Krishna, and Mohammed, it becomes quite clear that in spite of some primary similarities, they were each quite different from all the others, each archetypal in a way.

That which is organic is mortal and that which is not organic survives continuously through a variety of mortalities—births, deaths, and changes in form. That which is not organic is also not mortal. The channel through which objective knowledge is communicated in the human realm dies when the body dies, although the field of communication does not die. That means that objective knowledge is stored or used someplace other than in the channel through which it is communicated. This is a very important consideration. Objective knowledge has to be transmitted, received, taken out of the channel it is received through and used or applied somewhere else. If objective knowledge stays in the channel of communication of observation or perception, it is of no ongoing use whatsoever. It, of course, has some very temporary possibilites. It is of no use because it will die when the body dies.

But if objective knowledge is communicated, received, and used properly, it will remain in effect and useful when the body dies. It will enter the "stream of continuum," the contextual field of creation. It will be productive and creative, even eternal.

The reason for organic communion, both sexual and otherwise, is to establish objective knowledge someplace other than in the organic being. To *use* the organic being as a vehicle to go *beyond* the organic being. Organic communion is not just to have cosmic experiences or transcendental pleasure. It is also to place information somewhere other than in the mortal realm.

Secret 56: The Cycles of Sexual Communion

Sex is the most powerful driving energy in the human condition, and sexual communion is the most fragile circumstance.

Sexual communion rests on Magic, and you can kill the Magic, easily. For instance, if you get righteous about having to have sex a certain way, you destroy the margin that allows sexual communion to be communion.

Sexual communion is not about hopping on your partner, "banging away" for two hours, having thirty orgasms, and becoming completely exhausted. (That's just good sex.) You can manipulate energy to have good sex...even cosmic sex...but you can't manipulate sexual communion because it rests on Magic, not on "pushbutton" bodies—like, "Plug dick in pussy...Zing." It doesn't happen like that once one starts working with the higher centers.

If there is no Magic in the relationship, then there can be no sexual communion. Everyday, people change—and within a relationship they don't necessarily change at the same rates and in the same ways. It's very difficult to keep Magic in a relationship—a most delicate and hard process. But it can be done...especially if one is willing to take the time.

When people ask me about tantra and sexual communion I say, "Have you been in a relationship for a couple of years? Show me a little discipline first." Sexual communion moves through cycles. The same three cycles that I have used elsewhere to describe the stages of spiritual work, also apply in every aspect of relationship. (For more about these stages see *Living God Blues* by Lee Lozowick {Hohm Press, Prescott, Arizona, 1984.})

When people make "breakthroughs," they move from the place they are at to a higher place, but they don't (cannot in fact), eliminate the laws of cycles. The onward transformation or evolution is like a constantly expanding spiral. Each cycle is energetically, or contextually, aligned to the previous one, but the specific form of the cycles does not change as one matures or moves on in the ongoing transformational process.

As an example, the most basic cycle is Infatuation-Indifference-Doubt. A couple, in the first blush of meeting and agreeing to be together, is blindly unaware (or in habitual denial) about those tendencies in each other that presage personality friction, future disagreements, or crises. (Hormones are just too insistent for most people to maintain clarity.) After a while, though, the thrill of discovery is overshadowed by the reality of the hard work of any deepening relationship (albeit full of joys for the mature individual). At this point, the individual's chronic refusal of life produces indifference. Then, the lack of nutrition and common delight of such an indifferent state leads to doubt.

If the doubt is worked with, as one of the opportunities for self-awareness and *sadhana*, this work will produce insight, the first aspect of the second cycle (Insight-Frustration-Remorse) in the evolving spiral. Insight moves on to frustration, which is the result of the impatience and urgency to "get on with it"—in conflict with the Universe's time schedule, among other aspects of frustration. You know you have hit frustration, in the second cycle, when there aren't any alternatives—when you wouldn't have any other relationship. (You know you are in the indifference of the first cycle when you are looking around and there are lots of alternatives to the relationship you are in.) Frustration is not about feeling that if it doesn't work out you will find somebody else. By this stage you realize that there *isn't* anyone else. What do you do if you are the only man and woman on the face of the earth? You've got no options; you're frustrated! (Of course, if you're a man you might think about finding a squirrel-hole in a tree, putting a little moss in it, and letting the sun shine on it after it's rained to get it steaming...and then....)

You are frustrated! The sex isn't working...there's personality clash..she wants one thing, you want another...you feel like you will never get it together...there are no alternatives...you aren't looking around: then you know you've hit the second cycle. You have to deal with the frustration, but not by going somewhere else. That's a level of real maturity in a relationship! That moves on to remorse for the inevitable tensions caused by frustration. And so on.

So, one starts with Infatuation-Indifference-Doubt, and that moves into Insight-Frustration-Remorse, which moves into Free Moment-Disposition of Unenlightenment-Compassion. And this progression takes time! You can "screw your bloody brains out" and you still won't get to that third cycle in a year. (You don't have to know how to tell when you are in the disposition of unenlightenment part of the third cycle, because by the third cycle you've already got knowledge!) If you dedicate yourself to a relationship, it usually takes a couple of years to work out some "kinks." Each pattern may cycle through a few times, depending on one's maturity in and dedication to Tantric practice. (One doesn't necessarily get through the first cycle, Infatuation-Indifference-Doubt, just once and then get Insight immediately.)

But, the Insight of the second cycle will create a very different type of Magic in your relationship. So will Compassion.

Secret 57: Jesus Was A Tantric Master

> Jesus said to them, "When you make the two one, when
> you make the inner as the outer and the outer as the inner,
> and the above as the below, and when you make the male and
> the female into a single one so that the male will not be male
> and the female not be female, when you make eyes in the place
> of an eye, and a hand in the place of a hand, and a foot in the
> place of a foot, and an image in the place of an image, then
> shall you enter the kingdom."
> —*The Gospel of Thomas (22:4-7)*

Now that hits the mark! It is incredible that Jesus said this,
and that it is not alluded to in the New Testament. By saying,
"When you make the two one..." he means, "When you see
through duality, when you see nondualistically..." Jesus was a
pure Vedantist. When you stop conceptualizing comparisons,
when you stop seeing individual things over and against other
things, then you will enter the kingdom.

Jesus was also a master of tantra. "When you make the male
and the female into a single one, so that the male will not be
male and the female not be female..." We could interpolate from
this (and insult all the Christians) saying that Jesus went to
India and Tibet and studied tantra. But even if he didn't, he
discovered, somewhere in his practice, the Essence of Tantra.
Tantra is a lot more than just sexual diddling in a ritual format.
Ramakrishna became a tantrika, but not the kind of tantrika
that went around teaching it to all his women disciples. Jesus

is saying to make the man as woman and woman as man. In working sexual tantra that is exactly what happens. The separate identity, based on the illusion of survival in any given (and mortal) form, ceases to hold our attention.

Women tend to lose themselves much more easily than men. The man, in his insecurity and rigidity, remembers that he's the one doing the "humping," or "getting humped." The man almost always keeps a little bit of himself reserved so that he can observe the proceedings. In mature tantra practice one doesn't even know (if I can be a little crude about it), if they are the one doing the fucking or the one being fucked. This is because the whole duality of that separateness is dissolved in a swirling union of forces. Sometimes one doesn't even know there's fucking going on. One may even forget if they are a man or a woman.

Gender roles are totally delineated for us from the minute we get our little blue or pink knitted beanies when we're babies. Our roles are culturally or socially defined. And then we come to this moment when we literally don't know if we're a man or a woman! It is a bit of a shock...don't you know?

What Jesus is saying is, "There are a lot of ways to go, ladies and gentlemen." He says you can do the Vedanta trip, the trip of nondualism. You can also go the route of "Neti, neti"—"Not this, not this." By saying, "When the outer becomes the inner..." he means that no single object, seen over and against any other object, is God. Then he says "When you make the male and the female into a single one, so that the male will not be male and the female will not be female, then you will enter the kingdom"... this is the tantric path. Then he says, "OK, if those three aren't up your alley, how about another one? 'When you make eyes in the place of an eye, and a hand in the place of a hand, and a foot in the place of a foot, and an image in the place of an image....' " So he's saying, "OK, how about just taking what you got? You don't know you've got an eye. When you make a real eye in place of what you think is your eye, that's pretty good. You might think you've got hands, but you don't know you've got hands. It's all ego. When you really know that this is a hand... when you make a hand in place of a hand...that'll get you there. That'll get you to the kingdom." Pure Zen! He's given his disciples four choices in terms of paths—four ways to go. They'll all get you there, but you've really got to do your sadhana. Pick which way you want.

Secret 58: In Awakened Consciousness
There is Only One

It is not sexual communion when two people look at one another and are just happy to be together. Sexual communion is when the chamber[10] that is created is one of complete awakened consciousness—i.e. when the two people involved are irrelevant. "Who they are" is even irrelevant because consciousness is completely awakened. That is what lovemaking should lead to.

There is the possibility of achieving that if two people enter into lovemaking with that idea in mind.

Now, one person can do it without the other, which is what tantric initiation is about. That is not the whole idea, but in tantric initiation the initiator can produce that effect in the other. The idea of the priestess in tantric work is that she *is* that consciousness already. She's like the spiritual Master. She can produce in the novice the mood of awakened, free consciousness.

If you are functioning with an awakened consciousness, the only object of your attention is what it is that needs the Influence of the Divine in that moment. You don't have an attention that scans. You have attention that is extreme and unwavering,

---

10 chamber - from 4th Way terminology. Not an actual room, or physical space, necessarily, but an energetic bond created between or among people for purposes of focusing attention in the accomplishment of some work, spiritual or otherwise.

because it is drawn to and locked in on what is needed in that moment based on your awakened consciousness.

Communion is the point. Certain chambers are only accessible when there is only "one"—a space of unity.

Sometimes you move into that "one-ness," that space of unity, randomly, arbitrarily. (You don't know how you got there, but when you are there it's great.) Sometimes, in order to approach that point, that which is "two" needs to be exhausted.

And sometimes the way you exhaust that which is "two" is by prolonged sex. But, that lovemaking can get very boring at a certain point. So, what do you do? You sex in the midst of boredom—the point being communion. If the alchemy is still happening, you'll find the machine becomes irrelevant, and then there is only "one" in the chamber.

Communion is the end result when there is only "one" in the chamber. Why? That's not our business. It may seem strange but it's not our business. It's the business of who feeds off what is produced when there is only "one" in the chamber. Whatever it feeds is the one that makes the law. We don't know why. I could come up with a lot of sophisticated metaphysical explanations, but none of them would be the point. The "why" is not our business. The *doing of it is* our business. Why is the doing of it our business? It's been given to us and the rewards are self-evident.

• • •

In the consideration of sexuality in a spiritual path, the question arises of whether the Tantric Revelation—of unity, or becoming one—happens inside or outside of oneself? Is the sexual Tantric Revelation a partner-realization, or is it exclusive to the individual's inner world?

In my view, unless this unity is realized inside oneself, any possibility of union outside of oneself is almost nil. On the other hand, once that unity does happen within oneself, any reasons for denying the true nature or manifestation of Enlightened Duality[11] (which includes sexuality), become nonexistent.

The ongoing dynamic in a relationship between a man and a woman, assuming that neither has discovered this union of essential polarities of male and female within themselves, provides an effective forum for them to discover that, both singly and as a couple.

The workability of this discovery is a matter of the willingness of both partners to make the realization of the actual science of polarity more important than personal issues of control and distraction.

---

11 enlightened duality - the stage beyond non-duality in which one is no longer under the illusion of separation from God but sees and appreciates the uniqueness and blessedness of ordinary existence, and uses the elements of creation as a means of on-going lovemaking with the Divine. This approach characterizes the Baul Path.

Secret 59: About Conserving Orgasm

There are two distinct relationships to tantric sexual work. In one, the man withholds ejaculation and the woman has as many orgasms as arise in the particular period of lovemaking without bringing the man to orgasm (unless it's a subtle, whole bodily orgasm). In the other: both the man and the woman refrain from orgasm and utilize the energy charge that is built up when the body and the psyche are demanding orgasm.

In the second type in which both people refrain from orgasm, they "edge" towards it and use the tension. They use the energy generated to stabilize at one level, and then they begin to work up to the next level. They keep working towards orgasm, stabilizing at a level of tension prior to orgasm, and then going on to the next level with intensity.

Tantric practice can be used to aid and abet the transformational process since its energetic dynamics can be essentially alchemical. But, to consider never having orgasm is artificial, exclusive and impractical. Both men and women, therefore, can begin practicing by conserving orgasm, not by eliminating it completely.

Try having no orgasm for one period of lovemaking, but not necessarily for every time. Experiment a little—don't get locked into one exclusive approach. There are circumstances in which, for the man, ejaculatory orgasm can serve a very specific purpose in the chamber that the couple is "journeying" in at the time. Not to have that would limit a range of possibilities.

232

It is understandable that both people may be a little scared and unsure in this domain of practice. For a lot of men the whole notion of conservation of orgasm is very strange. The first couple of times they do not have orgasm it may be by accident. They may read books on tantric energy and try it, but at first the inspiration may not really be there.

In this experimental process it's very important to respect one another's responses. Sometimes a fraction of a second really makes a difference! The right timing may allow one to sustain the peak just prior to orgasm long enough for the body to calm down so that more active lovemaking may begin again.

To respect one another's responses doesn't mean to be tensed up, however. The woman should not be so afraid to move, the whole time, so that the man doesn't ejaculate. But, on the other hand, if she just goes wild, that is hardly being responsive to her partner.

You don't have to sit down ahead of time and talk it out. In general, you can simply have the disposition or agreement, before you go into lovemaking, that you are going to experiment with transformational sexual energy. Then your radar is "on" and you can go at it.

I also recommend that both men and women, but particularly women, consider the possibility of the energy of orgasm going in and through the body—through the nervous system—instead of just going out. Consider that the energy can literally reverse itself, almost like being recycled.

(I do not recommend using pressure points to forestall male orgasm. A pressure point at the perineum can either delay male orgasm or recycle semen into the bladder. It's a very popular technique in many tantric books, but I don't recommend it, although it works technically. I do recommend an energetic process between partners.)

If a man considers that orgasm can happen in an internal way without ejaculation, he can be in a much more patient and lasting communion with a woman without being plagued by the psychological need to ejaculate. Although it may begin in the genitals, internal orgasm, for both men and women, is not localized. And, once experienced, such orgasm will actually be much more desirable. In fact, after one or two experiences of internal orgasm, the psychological demand for genital orgasm will practically be eliminated. The demand will still arise occasionally (because it's damned persistent), but not regularly and consistently every time once you've discovered how to turn the energy inside, or how to move together through one another's cycles.

When the orgasm is internalized, there is not a relaxation after the implosion. The whole body is actually more "wired," in a pleasurable way. With implosive orgasm, the body is peaking without stopping. (And sometimes it's actually uncomfortable, rather than pleasurable.) The resolution is that the energy becomes fuel, so that you "travel." Whereas, with the explosive orgasm, you relax, and you haven't "gone" anywhere else.

Communion is the point. It doesn't matter whether the communion comes in the process of conservation of orgasm or from not having orgasm...from fifteen minutes of sexual play or from three hours. What matters is being in communion.

The partners can each work independently with their own internal energetic cycle, or together with the common cycle of man and woman. If the man and the woman work independently, the sexual play is like a generator that they are both plugged into. If they work together with the common cycle of man and woman, then the two points of contact in the body are the genitals and the face. The energetic connection can be mouth-to-genital or genital-to-genital. (It really doesn't matter.) The facial contact points can come from gazing into each other's eyes, or from breathing in a synchronous pattern in which the energy is connected. It can be the joining of mouths, breath, eyes. (I suppose it could even be third-eye contact, but I prefer something a little more familiar. I suppose if you are a third-eye mystic and every time you meditate your third-eye vibrates and talks to you, then this is more viable.)For most of us who are not constantly immersed in yogic third-eye phenomena, the eyes, breath, and mouth will be the contact points, along with the genitals.

If one is locked in mouth-to-genital contact, it's useful for both people to be joined that way in order for the male-female cycle to be optimally connected. When connected genital-to-genital, one person can be kissing the other person's neck while that other can be breathing in a particular pattern, and the connection will still be maintained. You can be literally face-to-face, but you don't have to be. (This can get humorous, but the mood is usually broken if one bursts out laughing. Then again, if you take this stuff too seriously, the tension in your body interferes with your attempts to surrender into one another.) You really want to be as relaxed as possible (although sometimes it's difficult because you are betting so much on this).

A woman may want to experiment with containing her orgasm just to see what her body does with that—just to see where it goes, and to follow what that energy will point to.

In any kind of sexual play, use instinct and follow the signals. Sometimes, instinct may say not to have an orgasm now, and at other times there will be no clear signals. When the signals are clear, however, follow them, if possible. At other times, both partners are really high, and the sex is just fantastic...but it's very clear that something is saying "slow down, stop moving, rest in one another, bond in one another, lie in one another's arms." But often, they really don't want to. They've been waiting for this night for a long time and don't want to give it up. But I would recommend that when the message is clear, follow the message. The clarity of the message is probably a result of having the right chemistry that night.

You will hit milestones in your sexual work together where you'll get to a certain point or plateau. You can stay at that point, which may be very wonderful, and have a very successful sexual relationship as far as it goes. But to stay at any point is to stagnate, and sooner or later deterioration will set in. So you are either growing, stagnating, or deteriorating. If you can keep growing, ideally even deterioration becomes growth. Death itself becomes "just another trip," instead of, "Oh no, I'm going to die!" For people who do not have the disposition to constantly grow, death is deterioration, and they will fight it with every weapon of their arsenal.

So you do come to milestones in sexual work. It doesn't necessarily mean that sex gets better or hotter. It may mean that the depth of your communion takes on a flavor that you've never had before.

You can't know what it is until you have had it!

● ● ●

Many women have been raised to believe that their job is to please their man. Advertising in the last 40 or 50 years has told women that their job, their sole reason for existence is to please their man (with the exception of having babies and cleaning house). A woman, therefore, will think that if she doesn't make the man ejaculate he will be dissatisfied and she will have failed in her job. There is a deep, primal, psychic program that says "...if he doesn't ejaculate he won't be happy and I will have failed as a woman."

In approaching conservation of orgasm, then, especially in the beginning (although it usually doesn't last for long), there may be a lot of hesitancy because the woman doesn't want the man not to ejaculate. If, as a woman, you analyze this hesitancy deeply enough, you will find that it stems from feeling incomplete, as I said, feeling like a failure. A woman may feel like that even if the man says, "I feel much better when I don't ejaculate. I'm enervated when I ejaculate. When I don't ejaculate my attention on you is stronger." There is a lot of essential insecurity in this domain.

It's a relatively easy process to avoid orgasm physiologically—the emotional and the psychological results of eliminating orgasm are the bigger thing that people have to deal with. This is predominantly true for men as compared to women, because women find it much easier to resensitize their bodies. Whereas men "need" genital ejaculation to feel like men! Therefore, the psychological adjustments necessary to beginning a practice of tantra are the most perfect opportunities for work on self. All the "crap" you've been hiding for years will start to come up. It's not so much about whether you "get it up" every night or not. Stuff like that is all superficial, and has to do with our self-image and how macho we are. The deep-seated knot in our sexuality, the primal stuff, has to do with ejaculatory orgasm.

For a man practicing non-ejaculatory sex, and once he has mastered the psychological urge, still, periodically, his body will cycle into a very strong urge to ejaculate (and as quickly as possible so he can go do something else). If the man passes that point, however, maybe 45-minutes to an hour into it, the body simply quiets down (unless he is "humping away" like crazy). But if he modulates his sexual activity, if he moves through the second urge to orgasm, then again his body will literally quiet down. Then there will be a tremendous leeway for movement— for sexual activity—beyond simply lying there so he doesn't ejaculate. Then another point will come...And so there is a cycle.

I don't know if this is true in women, but each point of the cycle for a man becomes harder to pass through. The first point becomes easy to pass through once you've dealt with the psychological issues, because the orgasm is very weak. But the longer you are in sexual communion—the more you feel the promise that the orgasm will blow every part of your body to the four corners of the room—the more demanding the urge to ejaculate is for a man. At each plateau the urge to orgasm will literally go away for a long while, and then all of a sudden it will be right there again, much stronger than the last time. And, for a man, the longer sexual play goes on the longer time there is in between these urges to orgasm(to ejaculate)—i.e. the time between the cycles extends itself.

• • •

There are different types of ejaculatory orgasm. If a man "cranks up" and then holds back, tensing until the orgasm is forced, the ejaculation tends to be very powerful, exhaustive, and then enervating later on. But if a man can relax into ejaculation, the orgasm is much different—and not enervating. The nervous system doesn't explode. There is simply a transfer of energy.

When, in particular circumstances, the physical chemistry of male and female fluids are necessary alchemical ingredients in the "experiment" (I'm speaking of something beyond the subtle energetics such as what love produces between man and woman), then explosive orgasm may produce the chemistry, but it will not allow the experiment to go on to its conclusion. It cuts the experiment off. Relaxing into ejaculation, on the other hand, will still produce the necessary chemistry without the explosive and enervating effects. When allowing ejaculation, a resting in one another's *being* tends to be physically sympathetic. Being together, the partners allow the physical chemistry to trigger subtle chemistry. They can let the alchemy infuse them and take them over, rather than doing anything to make it happen.

• • •

In China around the time of the 12th and 13th centuries, the upper class men were involved in polygamy, and many of them had twenty or thirty wives, concubines, and servants. There was a very exact science in which the male head of the household had to "service" all of the women in the household. Without ejaculating he would draw in their yin forces. At a certain point in the month, having accumulated all of the yin force from all of the other women, the man was supposed to be with the first wife. He was to ejaculate with her, and she was supposed to be trained in using all of the yin force built up over the preceding month from all of the other women. So, in one view, a certain amount of energy is built up, and then there is discharge that actually conveys the energy.

I view it a little differently, however.

The exoteric description of non-ejaculatory sex for the male is that the man engages sexual play with the woman and unites his energy with her energy. There are two versions of this. One: he brings the woman to a certain point, he then ejaculates, the woman's fluid mixes with his, and then he literally draws the fluids back up—physically, muscularly. In the other version: the man engages sexual play with a woman and their union builds up a certain charge which he draws up psychically or subtly. In this approach—the conservation of ejaculation—the charged semen rises up the spine to the brain. From the brain it chemically alters certain glandular secretions and filters back down into the body.

There is tremendous disagreement about whether that process is a physical or a subtle one, but I tend to lean toward the subtle process theory—that the man and woman reach union, and then they exchange energies. In the exchange there is a point of alchemical transmutation in which the energies cease to be essentially male or female. In this case, both the man and the woman, equally, are available to the benefits of that energy; whereas in the other case, the man draws all the woman's yin and she's left just being the generator or the reservoir, so to speak.

The body fluids of both the man and the woman do play a role in the energy exchange. Actually, they are even vital to it. But, after the exchange of energies, these physical fluids become secondary. For instance, once its purpose has been served the semen is dead substance and can be discharged. (It's just a theory, but that's the way I view it.)

Now the important part, of course, is to make sure that there has been this real exchange of energy. The substances themselves don't become divinized. They become divinized up to the point at which there is a transmutation of energy, at which time there is a shift from the physical to the subtle. The key is making sure that the transmutation has taken place, because as in any alchemical ritual, if the substance is expressed or discharged before the transmutation has taken place, basically the experiment is ruined and you have to start all over. It is like when healers spend weeks and sometimes months perfecting certain medicines or potions. One mistake, and months of work can go completely down the drain, the formula rendered useless. In the same way, if ejaculation occurs before completion of the process of transmutation, then what has been begun is useless. It hasn't meant anything. You only get the effects if you complete the cycle. If you don't complete the cycle, basically no harm is done, but there is no benefit either and you simply remain where you are.

• • •

Due to primal fear, at the moment of death a certain "essence" is released. In the language of Fourth Way (Gurdjieffian) work, this is called "food for the moon.[12]" So, for example, the "moon"

---

12 Feeding the moon - The idea, as expressed by George Gurdjieff, which relates to "feeding" the survival-oriented force of the separative nature of creation, as opposed to "feeding the sun"—the Work, through surrender to the Will of God and alignment to the Great Process of Divine Evolution. See: *In Search of the Miraculous* by P.D. Ouspensky.

likes war because so many people die and such a huge banquet is released. The "moon" likes the struggling and the cries of anguish—a feast of death. The most valuable thing the "moon" gets from human beings is what they release emotionally when they are in states of survival. So if you have gone beyond that survival mode, then the "moon" is not particularly interested.

Some people call orgasm "little death." If you're a man and you're smart, you "die" every time you have sex with a woman, whether you have ejaculatory orgasm or not. And if you're a woman and you're smart, you "die" every time you have sex, and such "death" automatically produces a greater life. By the time you are old and your body is fully ready to die, therefore, you won't be "feeding the moon" any more because you will have already transformed your ability to work for the Divine. Death will be a process you have learned how to use, instead of an affront to your position or stance.

Using "the moon" as an analogy for woman: a woman won't be interested in manipulating, dominating, or mothering a man if he "dies" when he enters her physically and spiritually. But if he doesn't, if he enters her as a conqueror, as an authority, as a scientist, then she's going to do her best to "kill" him.

The principle of working with male/female polarity is at play here. Men who feel they can't trust women feel that way because they aren't willing to die in a woman's arms, metaphorically speaking. They are, quite simply, terrified of the vision of themselves which such a "dying" would afford.

So men have a much greater task than women to perform. All women have to do is relax into who they are. But men, relatively speaking, have to become something entirely other than what they are. Dealing with the polarity of Shiva/Shakti in this way is "what to do until the Messiah comes."

Secret 60: Women: Put Your Orgasm in Your Eyes

Some women think they have to thrash around and wail, to be as active as they can, for a man to be satisfied in sex. Other women, of course, are terrified to even make a peep. (And if women are terrified to peep, men are paralyzed.) But, truthfully, it is possible to have an orgasm, to have "your brains blown to every corner of the universe" and yet not move. It is possible to reach the height of ecstasy without leaking energy. (In fact, that wailing and thrashing activity generally obstructs 90% of the possible sexual experience; it obstructs the body and distracts attention from the higher centers.) Given enough time, all mountains end up being valleys. The best sex is found in the valley, not at the peak.

Women know that men don't like a dead fish. And believe me, they don't! Most men don't like a dead fish unless it's sushi. But there is a higher possibility of sex, and that communication takes place in the valley. There can be as much communication that comes through the eyes, throat, hands, or the thighs, as there is through wild thrashes or screams. The right kind of moan is worth a thousand screams. That doesn't mean you should never let your body go, but to fall into the neurotic rather than natural urge is to reenforce life-negative patterns.

That first body flash can be pretty big. But if you allow a certain tension to build in the body, the peak available in the first orgasm will seem like a valley compared to the peak developed when that tension is maintained.

It is not a matter of never screaming or moving, or always lying there. Just lying there doesn't serve communion either. But imagine if you were to take what your body wants to do and put it into your eyes. Women are always asking, "How can I serve my mate, my partner?" We've talked about the principle of a man becoming Woman. Well, the easiest way for you as a woman to help a man to become Woman, when you are having sex with him, is to put your orgasm in your eyes. When he sees that, it will make such a communication that he will be your slave. Fifteen years of talking alone with him will never touch the communication made when you put that in your eyes. If a man sees that in a woman's eyes once, it makes up for 15 years of, "We've gotta work this relationship out..." "You've got to open up..." "I understand how hard it is for men..."

Secret 61: Become A Consort for Your Partner

The word *consort* is often used in a less than technical sense to indicate a woman who has a relationship to a man who already has a primary relationship with a wife. The consort then is "the other woman,"..."on the side." Actually, that is a sloppy use of the term.

More precisely, a sexual consort is a woman whose center of gravity[13] is stabilized at the fourth (or heart) chakra or above. A woman couldn't be a consort, in this technical sense, without her center of gravity being that high because she wouldn't have the necessary focus. She would be too distractable. One of the consort's functions, in this specific use of the word "consort," is to pull a man's center of gravity up. A consort could be one's wife or a ritual female partner who has the training to establish a movement of energy in a man for the center of gravity to move up. A consort, therefore, has value to a man whose center of gravity is below hers, or equal to hers but not stabilized. (If the man's center of gravity were above the woman's, then he would be her consort.) In a marriage, each partner could be a consort for the other at various times and in various moods.

It's not that the consort herself pulls the man's center of gravity up and does the stabilization. Rather, that's what happens based on her Being—on who she is in relationship to the Divine.

---

13 center of gravity - the "place" or point in the energy-body or chakra system from which one's responses to situations are generated. "Where one lives."

Geishas were trained in a way which enabled them, by choice, to move their center of gravity up or down. They were very much like *yoginis*. They would choose where to "center" their attention; therefore, the center of gravity would never sink all of a sudden or by surprise.

If the man had his center of gravity essentially stabilized in the fourth chakra or above, there would be no need for a sexual consort. However, one's spiritual Master could always be considered a consort of a special kind, as would the Divine Beloved. One seeks, longs, yearns to be in unending and unbreakable communion with this special Consort. The Sufis call this *Ruin;* the Bauls call this realizing union with *Maner Manush,* the Man of the Heart.

What enables a woman to move her center of gravity to a higher level is surrender to the body of knowledge to which she is apprenticing—that is, being in communion with her consort, her Beloved.

Every woman should be a consort to her man, so this discussion applies to every woman.

Invisibility is crucial to the woman's ability to do what it is that the consort does. Lack of invisibility muddles the process. Invisibility is the capacity to communicate what it is that your function serves with no fuzzy edges, no hidden agendas, no strings attached. The consort's function doesn't have to do with relationship, or sex, or higher sex, or cosmic sex. It doesn't have to do with love or submission to her man. It has to do with energy. It has to do with the issue of masculine/feminine polarity, and the kind of energy balance and interchanges that the masculine/feminine dynamic of polarity embraces. A consort must be invisible because energy dynamics are purely impersonal. The lowest end of the spectrum is pure instinct, procreation of the species, and the highest end is the literal creation of woman out of man—the ultimate Shakti/Shiva play in which Shiva actually becomes Shakti. Feminine energy comes out of the matrix of man. This is found in the mythology of all the traditions if you go back far enough. The job of a consort is to isolate and define, and then enliven certain aspects of male/female polarity.

When a woman is both a consort and a mate, the times in which she is being a consort need to be defined. A woman would not want to be invisible all the time or she would be completely impersonal with her man, and there would be no relationship.

Ideally, women will be like chameleons—invisible when invisibility is required and visible when visibility is required. There is no decision to change colors; the woman simply changes colors instinctively based on the environment. And, that is obviously a very high state of consciousness.

A consort can work with three patterns of energy. First, with the Power Center (sexual center)—defining, clarifying and establishing the pattern of energy here. For instance, if one night it feels like the Power Center should be worked on, invisibility means that the man and the woman move into sexual communion with only the idea of serving the Power Center in its evolution. There should be no looking into one another's eyes and thinking how beautiful the other one is, and no consideration for one another's comfort, discomfort, smell, appearance. The entire focus should be the Power Center.

The second way a consort can work is by raising the center of gravity; that is, moving energy from base to crown chakra. And, this too can be done through sexual exchange.

The third pattern of energy a consort can work with has to do with being a Man or Woman. (It is not necessary to have a consort to do this kind of work, but the role of a consort can be helpful.) Instead of melting into a man in some cosmic, Shiva/Shakti union, a consort can define man from woman, clearly.

You should never get too righteous about these things, however. A mate who is also a consort needs to know when to just "get laid" and when to be a consort. For a woman who is in a coupled relationship with a man, there are times in which sex is just sex, and there are times in which it's not just sex. It gets very tricky.

Secret 62: Man as a Conduit for a Woman

The Goddess *is* the universe; so, ideally, a woman doesn't need a man to tap into the universe. She is the universe.

But, if a woman can't entirely access who she is as a Woman; if, in sexual communion for instance, she is not able to access her own feminine, then the man can be her socket to the juice from the universe. A man can cycle a woman back to herself.

The way a woman uses that possibility is to hold that intention. You hold the concept that in sexual communion the man is a conduit for energy, life, revelation, communion, transcendence. You simply rest in that, which doesn't mean peering at him and imagining him to be this big tube leading out to the universe somewhere. There are too many traps to fall into using creative imagery, or creative meditation, in such forms.

Instead, simply language it to yourself that your partner is being a conduit to these things, and then hold that intention as a possibility.

Secret 63: Adoration and The Mood of Woman

A woman gains her life through a man's adoration, and her life gives him life. In very crude terms (i.e. in terms of the lowest, common denominator), an unadored woman, a single female human being, is a piece of dead meat, but adoration brings Life. That is the way it works, but you need to have *Draw No Conclusions Mind* about this, because it's not what it sounds like. Adoration doesn't mean that before sex a man burns a stick of incense and bows to the woman in some empty gesture. Adoration has nothing to do with blatant false holiness. It is not a subject-object relationship. That is the way it appears, but it's not like someone of the male gender worships someone of the female gender. Adoration has to do with losing self-reference in God-reference. (Put another way, adoration has to do with the recognition that one is never without the Work, or never out of view or out of regard of the Divine.)

The Goddess is what's Real, and tranformational work is what we do that we think is going to get us there. So, Woman *is* the Work, in our language here. One's relationship to that— relationship to the Work—should be one of profound gratitude and awe. And as gratitude and awe mature, the ultimate form will be adoration.

In approaching the true understanding of adoration, attention is where one begins. (This discussion will reach a more nondualistic level before we're done, but in the interim....)

When a man and a woman get together, they need to

attentively serve one another. Lovemaking demands total unwavering attention. But, the usual man's sex is not lovemaking itself, because by conditioned, subconscious definition, sex is exclusively genitally oriented. By neurotic psychological definition, sex means genitals, intercourse, orgasm, domination, manipulation and at core, separation. That's why sex is not lovemaking. Lovemaking begins where this kind of sex ends.

• • •

Harry Chapin, the man I consider to be *the* genuine balladeer of our time, was an objective artist. His music touches all of the centers of your being. Unfortunately, he died several years ago in an auto accident. One of Chapin's songs, *Corey's Coming,* is about the shamanistic placing of attention.

If a man's attention is habitually, without consciousness, drawn to a woman or anything feminine, or to pornography, immediate orgasmic release, or to any object for that matter, he can never place his attention with intention and focus. To place attention optimally, one must be able to see how his attention is drawn automatically (a function of distraction, fascination, or neurosis), and must manage that attention. Even if the interest is organic—if, for instance, you have a lot of juicy, sexual energy and haven't had a partner for years—still you must be able to consciously place your attention as if you were awake, not asleep. If you can't, you'll be drawn by what the Buddhists call "desire," which, according to the second law of the Buddha is the cause of all suffering.

To be able to manage your attention you must be willing to live alone. Not that you will necessarily end up doing so, but if you are not willing to, it will be impossible to control your attention, to place it in its home—its right place. There must be no limits, no expectations, and no fixated or narrow ideas of what this management of attention will produce. Otherwise, you will be continually fascinated and seduced, and you'll have no ability to resist the attraction of those things that promise you the fulfillment of your desires (which to ego means Heaven) or the non-fulfillment of your fears or resistances. Every shaman is willing to live alone. Most rarely ever do, but they are willing to.

No matter how much sexual energy a man has, he doesn't, essentially, need a woman as a mate. That doesn't mean that it's not a perfectly appropriate, wonderful, even world-shattering event to be mated to the proper person. But a man does not *need* a woman. Man needs Woman, but that is a horse of a different color, a skunk of a different stripe, a fish of a different scale. Yep, you betcha.

A man who is irresistible to women is a man whose interest in a woman cannot be detected, that is, a man who is his own person, who rests in his Being. If a woman cannot tell whether or not a man is interested in her, the man might say only one word, and, with rare exception, she'll fall all over herself for him. A woman knows that a man like this can place attention and therefore can truly worship her as her objective Feminine longs for—with Adoration, Real Adoration, not "a" man's neurotic attachment to her as an individual personality/psychology unit.

Sometimes by accident a man who cannot place attention will really touch a woman, but basically he will just sex her and have an orgasm, then roll over and go to sleep, or have a cigarette, or bounce out of bed saying, "I'm starvin', how 'bout you?!" Or, he might just be like a typical five-year-old looking for mommy. You know the type—the life of the party—who jumps, or flys out of bed three seconds after orgasm (his, that is) and yells with disgusting enthusiasm, but often endearing naivete, "What do ya say, I'll make you an omelette...your favorite omelette, tomatoes and cheese, huh, huh?!"

Half of them do that, and the other half fall right asleep. So take your choice.

●　●　●

Attention does not mean staring at somebody. If you're staring at somebody, your mind is going to be too busy fantasizing,
too full of mental gyrations to have total unwavering fixation.
One fixates one's attention with other than the physical senses.
If the physical senses spontaneously interplay, that's one thing,
but you can't get there through the physical senses. You cannot get to unwavering fixated attention by staring, or thinking
one-pointedly, or concentrating on your sitting in meditation—
with every breath perfect. "Concentration, concentration, don't
waver." It doesn't work that way.

To adore Woman, one can follow the "scent" of Woman in
one's partner. But, that lead is not necessarily given consciously.
It is a very unusual woman who will know the true direction
to give, and be able to give it consciously. A woman gives directions when she is "relaxed into." A woman's body, *the* body, is
always giving direction, often in complete antagonism to personality, psychology, posture, and even what passes for consciousness. It's Woman who gives direction, not "a" woman's mind.

To get direction from a woman, you need to find Woman, and
that is not necessarily the one who tells you to put the toilet
seat down, put the top back on the toothpaste, and throw your
dirty clothes in the hamper instead of leaving them all over the
bedroom. That one couldn't give you direction if you were sitting at one end of a table and asked which way to the other end.
So, it is important to recognize *what* gives direction.

How one lets Woman give direction is also by relaxing one's
own dynamic and allowing Her to call. If a man and a woman
are making love, and the only thing a man can think about is
his own process, he's not letting Woman show him anything.
There's no room in that kind of self-absorption. For a man to
let Woman give him direction, he's got to relax into what she
is always saying as Woman—not the woman's voice, not her

252

experience, not her emotions. It's what she says *as essential Woman.* If a man knows this, then he can follow, because Woman is always giving direction.

A woman's greatest cues to the path through the labyrinth[14] are not when she's cranking up to have an orgasm. No hints are given when a woman is wailing. That's what she does in between giving you the real hints. Men think, "Ah, now I'm getting somewhere. She's panting... Okay, the gates are about to open." The woman is screaming, "Ahhhh, ahhhh, ahhh, oh Jesus, oh God, ahhhh..." It is not those gates! Those are in another domain. It's when a woman completely relaxes that the hints are given. She tells with her breath, her posture, her eyes.

Who she *is* is always giving direction. Who she thinks she is is usually too busy trying to give what she thinks is direction to let the direction that Woman is always giving predominate and come through clearly. "In silence, and only in silence, will you know Me." That doesn't just mean a lack of speech. A woman's hints are in silence, and sex is the lowest or the grossest metaphor for what we are talking about. (Through sex as a metaphor, however, you could realize "As below, so above." You can realize the higher through the lower.)

Adoration allows a woman to see who she *is,* and when she sees who she *is,* she has found herself.

Some women will not relax. Silence is out of the question when a woman is too insecure, too disturbed. Some women's bodies are so in their way, full of tension and stress, that unless the body is "fed" a little bit, stroked, satisfied, it won't cooperate. On a very practical level, a lot of times people will take these flashy tantric workshops, and they will be told to always stay at the edge and never have an orgasm. For a few men or

---

14 labyrinth - the maze of the mind which metaphorically surrounds the "heart of the labyrinth" or the condition of surrender to the Will of God; a descriptive term used by Mr. E.J. Gold.

women that works well, but for many, they will never get to possibility that way both because they cannot sustain the silence there and because their bodies are too full of dissonance. They need an orgasm or two just to clear away some of the shit...and then it's too late; then they can't be bothered.

Before a woman's body can be her gateway, to what she doesn't even know she is looking for, her mind has to stop. If a woman's conclusions and considerations in the midst of physical lovemaking won't or don't stop, her body will never open the doors completely. A woman's mind stops, I suppose, for a few seconds during orgasm. Beyond that, women's minds can also stop during long periods of relaxed communion in lovemaking. Then a woman's body will show the man everything he needs to know, lead him to his destiny. But as long as her mind is "on," even if her mind is on pleasing him or serving him, it will not effect the Divine result. If her mind is on, her body will be responsive to her mind and not to its own Organic Innocence. If a woman's body is responsive to its own Organic Innocence, it will show a man everything. (A man sometimes gets a glimpse during a woman's orgasm, but it is one of those fleeting flashes that is never substantial enough for the man to follow. Not that it couldn't be. Academically, man could leap into that space in a matter of a second or two, but he's usually so busy thinking about what a big deal he is because of how strong she's "coming," that he couldn't possibly find the gate, or see the door when it opens.)

If the woman gets frustrated because the man isn't a "Real Man," she's missed the point. A woman has to make a man a Real Man by helping him bring her to life. And being brought to life as a woman is just the first step. Once one is brought to life, then they can get about doing something that really means something.

This mood of lovemaking, real Lovemaking, begins to permeate other areas of life; all of life itself. When that starts to show up sitting across the dinner table from her...when that starts to show up in the car driving to the movies with her...when that starts to show up under social occasions...it's going to be so antagonistic to the matrix of ego that usually runs things, that ego will try to kill this mood of Woman as soon as it shows up. Even knowing what it is and remembering where it's coming from, ego will try to kill it. That is why one needs to have a developed ability to bring intention, discipline, and attention to moment-to-moment practice. This is true for a woman too. When this mood starts to show up in a woman's life, it'll be just as threatening for her as for a man. It's non-gender-specific ego that is threatened.

The mood of Woman relates to feelings and not thoughts. The mood of Woman thinks, but it is stream-of-consciousness thinking, not demanding. Feelings demand, but the mood of Woman is always full. If a woman resting in this mood gets horny and wants to have sex, she will enjoy it, and at the same time it will not make any difference if she has sex or not, because she is already satisifed. There is nothing and no one to be satisfied. There is just satisfaction. Woman is already satisifed. When one feels that satisfaction then their stomach, or their genitals, or their eyes, or their ears won't rule them. The Work will rule, not the elements of personality or psychological makeup. But it takes some time to trust that kind of ecstasy.

One can develop a form that looks like this mood by eating nothing but apples and pears for several months, like some fruitarians I saw once. The woman looked like she was floating in bliss, but she was actually quite ill. The form approximated the Mood of Woman, the way we're describing it now, but that mood is infinitely more than a mere shell.

This description of the qualities of the Mood of Woman could apply to a description of the disposition of enlightenment. Woman is the Work. Enlightenment is the Work. Therefore, enlightenment is Woman. (Well, my trigonometry was never great, although I did get pretty good grades at it.)

• • •

If one doesn't relate to a woman as she thinks she is, even if the way she thinks she is is inaccurate, then there's no possibility for eliciting Woman. It's not about catering to every whim and wish of neurotics, but one has to recognize who she thinks she is and take that into consideration in relationship. We have to begin where we are, not in some fantasy of possibility. We are all at partial levels of development and maturity, and we need to serve both one another's immediate work as well as the "big picture."

• • •

Adoration is not something that can be consciously done, even with the best of intentions, but it is something we can dispose ourselves towards. We can optimize the possibility of it's arising—which is what we are talking about in practical terms.

One need not engage a relationship between a man and a woman in order to discover this. Neither should one not.

The relationship between a man and a woman is exactly analagous to the relationship between "being[15]" and "the machine[16]." One doesn't have to be in a relationship to observe men and women. If one is in a relationship, observation can be more acute, but then also there can be more obstacles. Observe men and women, not just in relationships—anywhere and everywhere. There are guys in every supermarket with big pot bellies and belt buckles half the size of their heads who think every housewife running down the aisle is going to think they are God's gift to womenkind. The swap-meet is another great place

---

15 Being - may roughly be equated with essence, the intrinsic nature of consciousness; also, a person's "presence."

16 Machine - the physical and subtle form of creation; as individuals, the subjective, survival-oriented body-mind.

to watch men and women. Go to the swap-meet and watch all the hippies, the men with long hair and no shirts on. Watch the way they relate to all the women who come and want to buy $2.95-turquoise-necklaces and think that they got a "real Native American bargain." Watch those kinds of interactions, and you're seeing men and women in action. Never mind the, "Oh yeah, but they're neurotic." Watch men's reactions to women mud-wrestlers, or, if you are a man and you want to take your life in your hands, go to one of the male striptease shows, although usually they don't let men in, and watch the women in the audience. Sit with *Draw No Conclusions Mind*. The answers to the question of distinctions between "being" and the "machine" are in those environments. But you have to be in those environments in the domain of possibility, not in the domain of rational perceptions. The less conclusions you draw, the more likely you are to be impacted, instinctually, by what you see.

The machine is our salvation, however. (In our language, and in alignment with the practice of the Bauls, we could say, "The Body knows.") We're not going to get to heaven by transcending the body but through the body. The job is to cease defining the body the way it has been defined by the illusions of ego and allow the body its organically innocent instinct. The task is not to somehow get some kind of subtle consciousness that will survive when the "junky, old body" dies. That's not the point. The body is the way. The body knows. The mind does not know.

Don't make the mistake of thinking of this consideration of adoration in terms of a man who has *being* relating to a woman, because that's not it. Consider *being* versus *the machine,* rather than "a being" in relationship to "a machine," and the information will be much more useful. We don't want to make the discussion personal. We want to keep it at the level of being and machine, not like "me and my mate," or "me and my friend." That principle (of being and machine) is what works. If we take the principle and define it personally in terms of men and women, it's going to become unworkable. At the same time, we are men and women, and this is what we've got to work with. The principle gets worked through us.

• • •

We are Woman, and it's the man in us that needs to adore that which we are, to bring what we are to life. Consciousness is masculine. Shiva is pure consciousness, is masculine. Shakti is the body. There's no Shakti without Shiva. Shiva brings Parvati to life. Parvati sits on Shiva's knee and says, "Great Master, I'm dead. How can I be brought to Life?" Shiva explains that to her, which is supposed to be what some of the *Guru Gita*[17] is about. The essential ground of Hindu mythology is man adoring woman and bringing her to Life. But Shiva doesn't adore Parvati in the way we think adoration happens. He's a great ascetic. He's in meditation so deep he doesn't even know she's sitting on his knee. He doesn't adore her by flapping his long silken eyelashes and being romantic or sentimental.

Shiva dominates Shakti, but from Shiva's perspective and from Shakti's perspective it's not domination. Only to the unenlightened mind, is it domination. It's like "Give in so as to conquer," the principle of Judo. In doing Judo, you don't give in to get thrown. You give in so your opponent will give in to meet you, and you end up on top. The best Judo player is the one who can surrender the best. The one who can give in the best gets to dominate in the end.

So too, in lovemaking a man throws himself at a woman's feet. For a woman to receive a man who has thrown himself at

---

17 Guru Gita - a long devotional chant in honor of the Guru, composed as a dialogue between Shiva and Parvati. Parvati asks Shiva about the principle of worshipping the Guru, and Shiva discourses about its transcendent possibilities.

her feet, however, her mind must go—one way or another. Mind must either open to embrace that man, or stop completely. Mind is the suit of armor, the veil, the wall.

So to summarize: First adoration, then Woman opens, then man is led. Woman follows man's lead first. Woman won't open unless she's adored. Man adores, woman opens. Man follows the opening—but he must be able to lead in order to follow.

Secret 64: Women Have Been Betrayed

When a woman is bathed in the light of adoration she does not awaken to her true Being instantaneously. Why not? Because she's grown up in a male-dominated, woman-crippling society. She's not going to easily drop thousands of years of proof that she will be brutalized and destroyed if she becomes real and juicy and vulnerable. And, she is one of her own worst enemies. She's aided man in his domination by forming herself into his image of her (or his demand for her). Just look at most of the "woman's" magazines these days! So, a woman is not going to be able to immediately come to honest terms with her own complicity in these matters.

And, who can a woman personally trust to awaken to Herself in relationship to anyway? Nobody! All her life, a woman has been betrayed by men, by other women, by advertising, by "Father Knows Best"-type TV shows... all of it. She's not going to just forgive and forget all of this right away. She can't.

So the man says, "Well, how do I need to be in order to awaken Woman in my mate?" And I say, "You need to 'kiss that woman's ass' for a long time! That is, you need to give her support, acknowledgement, time to heal and to feel into her essence as Woman."

"But," he says, "You don't know what it means to do that. She's always bossing me around. She's so neurotic, and she'll 'shop' me into the poor house," and so on.

If a man wants the woman he is in intimate relationship

with to awaken, he must bathe her in adoration for as long as it takes. He must "mid-husband" her until she gets out of the deep, deep habit of keeping herself invulnerable from that which has, in the past, always attempted to destroy her, suck up her energy, take advantage of her and enslave her.

This consideration can be applied to younger girls coming into womanhood also. Our responsibility is not to betray them as their mothers and grandmothers have been betrayed. And we need to bring this responsibility into the most practical domains by not being arbitrary in discipline, not telling them you're going to take them out to the movies if you aren't, not pacifying them by promising them future things that you won't give them. Keep them innocent as long as possible. Let them know how beautiful and alive they are without being sickly-sweet sentimental or manipulative. Don't feed them on the lies (the marketing strategies) of the patriarchial establishment. Support and embrace natural childbirth, nursing of children, and natural appearance.

We must show young women, by example, what a life of acknowledgement and honor is. If young women see relationships change every month, or if they see their mother (or father) in four different relationships in a year, that's essentially the dynamic they are going to enact. And the minute they start enacting that they're going to be betrayed—wounded in a life-negative way. They are not going to get constancy, adoration, happiness, or satisfaction. Instead, they will get misery, frustration, and disintegration.

The woman has a responsibility in relationship to being adored, and in relationship to her own awakening. She needs to be able to make distinctions between a man's true adoration, and his fawning, charming, flirtation. If a woman feels like she's being truly adored, truly respected for who she is, essentially, then it's a matter of focusing on that and not blaming her adorer for the past history of the entire male race.

It is very hard not to blame every individual man for all men. Women have developed habitual defense mechanisms because they've had to. A lot of this dynamic is not so much recoil or essential man-hatred as it is self-preservation. However, if a woman focuses on the adoration rather than on social past history, distinctions can be made relatively easily. To do otherwise is to continue to blame all whites for the slavery and brutality they caused blacks, to continue to blame all Germans for Hitler's atrocities, to continue to blame all Christians for the pogroms of the Jews.

Psychologically, a woman will want proof that the man's adoration is not temporary, and that as soon as he "gets the goods"— meaning sex, money, or whatever a man wants from a woman— he won't stop adoring her. Of course, if the adoration is real, a man won't want any "thing" from a woman except to see her awakened Being, to see her alive. But this must be shown over time. Under ordinary circumstances, she wants proof.

Secret 65: Transcending Sex

Orgasm is not the end result of intercourse, or shouldn't be. You go on from the urge to orgasm. That's transcending sex. Then you transcend love, if you allow the process to continue to expand as it will if it follows the natural energetic evolution. And what you will find, I'm sorry to say, which probably will be a great shock to some of you, is that you will tend to outgrow sex as you know it. It doesn't mean that at certain times and in certain specific moods you won't do it, you will simply tend to outgrow the usual motives, the narcissistic gesture of untransformed sexuality. Ideally, when you're overflowing with the bliss of real Life, sex is a random relationship you have with your beloved, but it's no more pleasurable than whatever else you're doing that's overflowing with bliss. It's a form of random relationship you have, specific to your mate or your lover. It's part of a natural relationship. But typically, sex is just a way of massaging a psychological need or cramp.

Why are we so into sex? Because of how it feels? Actually, it is because we die somewhere in it. We die in sex, and that's what we're looking for. We want to die desperately, to end our suffering. We want to be born again desperately, to feel. We want to wake up desperately. That's the big attraction in sex. It's not that it's genuinely any more important than anything else that takes place in real spiritual life. Real spiritual life is what is going on at the time, lived consciously and objectively. If what is going on is that you're sitting at the movies, sex is not more important than that. If what is going on happens to be sex, then it's sex.

What you will find is that you will tend to outgrow sex as you know it—as a release, as pleasure, as a high point of the evening or day, as afternoon delight, as the way you manipulate or are manipulated. Sex will tend to take its place along with everything else in your life, as a natural and spontaneous response to the moment. It will have its place in the instinctually appropriate time and place, mood and attitude. As it is, sex is not free of tensions. That would be interesting if it were. It's a big item. But you will tend to have sex naturally become a simple, relaxed aspect of relationship when you're practicing Tantra, which is a long way down the road for most people. That happens more towards the end of mature practice, not at the beginning.

When sex is seen for what it really is, which is communion with the Goddess or communion with God, depending upon whether you're man or woman, then the pleasure you derive from sex becomes grounded in reality. It doesn't become completely blown out of proportion to reenforce the need for more sex, for psychological "strokes." And you can go on from there because there is more. There is much more involved in communion with your lover than simply the act of intercourse and orgasm. Even when the act of intercourse and orgasm is accompanied by emotional feelings of pleasure, happiness, attention, there is still more, but you can't get on to more until you've been grounded in reality in terms of what's going on for your body and cells. You've got to ground your nerve endings in reality first, and then you can go on to what's more. As long as your nerve endings are hysterical, you can't be grounded in reality.

A funny thing about being grounded in reality is that you don't think about being grounded in reality. When you're doing it, you don't know it. It is just ordinary. It's the same thing in sex. You don't think, "Boy, that was a good one." You just get lost in it. And there's more. So, first you need to ground what's going on in reality before you can get to more.

Sex must become love, and love must be transcended. Intercourse does not have to stop. You don't have to transcend intercourse, but you must transcend the usual mechanical or habitual reasons for sex. Sex must become love, and love must be transcended. What transcends love? God. Sex turns into love, but to love you need the duality of lover and beloved. And even that must be transcended. You must lose the one who is loving. You must lose the one who is in love. So even sex that has been transformed into love, which is a beautiful thing, must also be transformed. The lover must be lost. So you, who are the lover, must lose yourself. You must transcend love and become the very nature of creation itself, which we call God. You must simply be what is going on as the Great Process of Divine Evolution. If what is going on happens to be sexual intercourse, that's what's going on. If what's going on happens to be verbal intercourse, that's what's going on. But the typical person, when verbal intercourse is going on, is doing in their head the other kind of intercourse, genital intercourse. So what must be transcended is not the form. What must be transcended is the search, the neurosis of genital absorption and exclusivity.

When you're sexing, just sex. Don't be busy interpreting every sound, every movement that's going on. Let your body do what it will. If two people are letting their bodies do what they will, they'll work perfectly together on the bed, on the floor, up the walls. When you're sexing, sex. Don't interpret, fantasize, invalidate, criticize, condemn, be guilty and all the other stuff that you do when you're sexing. You don't do that when you're seeing. When you're seeing, you're seeing. You aren't busy being guilty because you see. When you're just sexing, you'll find you will transcend sex. You will literally transcend it, because there is more. There's a lot more, but first you have to be doing what you're doing.

PART VI

Approaching God

In this concluding section the ultimate "secret"—the consideration of Loving God[1]—is indicated. This profound doctrine, the ultimate teaching of Lee Lozowick's work, has been alluded to throughout the entire text, but nowhere stated with the poignancy and directness that he uses in these final pages.

---

1 Loving God - the specific condition of having been taken beyond union with God to ecstatic relationship with God as "other," described by Lee Lozowick as the ultimate human possibility in his book, *The Only Grace Is Loving God*. A more ordinary usage refers to our innate devotional attraction and alignment with the Divine, which is our underlying, though unconscious, condition.

Secret 66: Longing Will Lead You To The Beloved

In a practical sense, Woman is the Beloved to a Man. Man's relationship to Woman is that of Shiva to Shakti. So a man seeks the Goddess, and when he finds anything less than the Goddess, he feels betrayed. As we've elaborated before, when a man doesn't know he's Man, but thinks he's just "a man," he instinctually wants to see Woman, but instead just sees the neurotic, greedy, envious, gossipy, jealous, possessive, territorial female, and so he feels betrayed.

What's a man's response to feeling betrayed? Anger. How does man express anger? Physical, verbal, emotional and psychic violence. The contemporary battle of the sexes, in fact, may not be the result of thousands of years of male domination and woman's need to find herself, but simply the result of man having closed eyes, of being unable to see deeper. A man lives in the dark. He doesn't know how to find Woman in a woman. He feels betrayed by not being able to see the Goddess in manifestation, so he attacks—through war, rape, violence, verbal abuse, and all of the forms of enslavement of women of the last couple of thousand years, and through bias, belittling, prejudice and so on.

To continue the analogy, it is entirely possible that we find the Beloved through longing. We recognize the Beloved by the lack of the Beloved's presence in our lives. Similarly, in our ordinary relationships as couples, and in a broader way with all relationships between the sexes, a man finds Woman through longing, recognizes Woman through the lack of Woman's presence. The human being is ruined and finds the Beloved not by union, but by lack of union with the Beloved, by longing for that. Perhaps one of the ways that a man can allow a woman to guide him through the labyrinth is not by attempting to make her animate the Goddess with every breath, which is impossible, but by being led by the pain of longing for that. Through the pain of longing for the impossibility of union with the Goddess, we may find the Goddess.

Secret 67: The Goddess and the Teacher

Here is a very practical way to look for the answers that are necessary to a life of compassion and alchemical transformation. You find a Teacher who lives and breathes...and bleeds and farts and burps, sometimes regularly and at other times irregularly...and who is, at the same time, the One who is, in essence, always making love to you, man or woman.

If one pierces the confusion and fear surrounding this, he or she won't have to do anything except receive the Goddess' Benediction, and follow Her. (Our disposition toward the Goddess can be the same whether we're men or women. Exactly the same.) Paradoxically, though, the Teacher is also the one who is simply the head of the exploratory party. The Teacher is the one with the most experience and the most acute "sixth" sense, and is leading the party through the labyrinth experimentally and by sense, without a map. The only reason one would follow this guide is because he or she is the one who is least likely to take the wrong path, the least likely to err or to weaken and be seduced.

It's still an experiment though. But here's a secret that is the key to the ability to "make love." One does not learn to make love. One can learn to make love in principle, but one won't, given all the elements of the formula of transformation. *Who one is* when they allow themselves to be made love to *is* making love in return. This is it. The big secret. But one has to be willing to be made love to by the Divine, by Her.

Secret 68: Devotion and Alchemical Transformation

The Bauls of Bengal, India, learned how to use devotion to generate alchemical transmutation. They even went beyond the Tantric Buddhist practice. The Bauls grew out of the Sahaja Buddhist sect (which was very active in India), the Vaisnava Hindus, and the Sufis. The Bauls took the essential philosophy of the union of male and female and the alchemical process that could initiate, and then went beyond the technical use of breath and muscular relationship. They brought devotion to a point where there was a similar energy exchanged, without the need to use all of the technical processes (not that they didn't use those anyway as a symbolic or archetypal manifestation).

I have generally been referring to sexual practice between a man and woman, but also, if the devotional aspect of transmutation were realized, an individual could practice in a way that would go beyond the gender consideration.

One would need to engage sexual play fairly often if the chemical process alone was followed, because the chemical process generally tends to be weak and in need of a lot of reinforcement in order to build up momentum and strengthen itself. But in a devotional process, union between a man and a woman could be infrequent and random and still utilize the chemical aspect, because the devotional aspect could actually carry the chemical process for a long time. The strength of the devotional process is superior to the strength of the chemical process.

If it's not obvious, that is one of the ways that this School is attempting to develop: with consideration of the chemical relationship between a man and a woman, but with a predominantly devotional matrix in which transmutation of sexual energy can produce the results that the tantrics sought.

Secret 69: Heartbrokenness and The Wound of Love

Humanity is suffering, and this condition has nothing to do with mistakes we've made. Maybe our mistakes have added a little bit of suffering in some domains, and maybe our successes have taken away a little bit in other domains, but life is suffering. That's what "heartbrokenness" has to do with, never with the past. Heartbrokenness has to do with what is now.

When you realize life is suffering, you also realize that there is only God—you realize the "Wound of Love"! So there is always the alternation between the "Wound of love" and the "heartbrokenness" of suffering: You feel and are empathic with the suffering of humanity, and at the same time you realize that at some level we are all absolutely absorbed or subsumed by Divine Influence.

When you know all life is connected, that opens the spring of love. You can't help feeling love when you feel the connectedness of all life—not just humanity, but also animals and plants and all other forms of existence. What else could you feel but love when there is nothing but existence? What else could you do but surrender to that? If, when you realized there is only God, you became empathic or telepathic to the collective unconsciousness of the human race, you would blow your brains out! You'd feel an unending deluge of psychosis and neurosis. But when you feel all of existence—the truth of life—and not just human beings, you feel love. You might weep or you might laugh, but you feel love. You can't feel that without also feeling that life is suffering. Without the absolute knowledge that "all life is suffering," as considered by Buddha, all you could feel is a weepy, sentimental subjectivity.

It's not about avoiding getting wounded. Most of us probably have things that we've resisted feeling all our lives because we think that we're supposed to somehow transcend the "Wound of Love" instead of allowing it to move us in a certain way. The game is to act based on the reality of the "Wound of Love": "This is the way life is. What can I do?" If one knows, one must do. All theorizing dissolves in the obviousness of the need to act according to alignment with the Great Process of Divine Evolution.

Women don't have to access the "Wound of Love." All women have to do is relax and it's right there—it's an active part of a woman's essence. For a man, it's more of a dormant part of his essence. So, once the "Wound of Love" is broken open in a man, then he has to learn to access it; learning to access it is simply a matter of consideration of the feminine. He can consider the qualities of receptivity and nurturing with all those with whom he would like to have a love relationship. Obviously, one wants that with as many people as possible, but we're more likely to focus on a mate, a child, a particularly close friend, or the spiritual Master. (Probably that's why grandmothers carry pictures of their grandchildren around with them. When the grandfather wants to access the "Wound of Love," the grandmother just takes out the picture of the grandchild and says, "Take a look at this, Henry. This'll fix you right up.")

There are certain stimuli that can be used to access the "heartbrokenness." If I need to do that, I just go to the supermarket and watch the way adults treat their children, then I am tortured to the point of true Feeling. That famous news picture of a Vietnamese girl running out of her burning village, or of the Ethiopian starvation, can generate that. Also, if you have personal experience, you can access it very easily. The longer you are in this Work, however, the less you will need personal experience. At some point, everybody's experience is personal experience.

Secret 70: The Consideration of Loving God

The consideration of Loving God must be an organic affair—it must express itself in your behavior. It doesn't have to do with understanding (understanding is just a function of the consideration), and it cannot stop with an intellectual analysis of the book, *The Only Grace is Loving God* (by Lee Lozowick, Prescott, AZ: Hohm Press, 1982). If you are not acting on the consideration of Loving God, then you aren't considering it. Your relationships with one another have to become the focus of your consideration of Loving God.

In order to consider Loving God, you must consider "loving," and you must consider "God." How do you consider "loving"? With other human beings. How do you consider "God"? With awe, respect, worship, and a sense that no knowledge or experience…none…is the Thing (God) itself.

While it is true that Loving God is essentially different from loving one another, at the same time, loving one another (or at least loving your mate or your child—which is loving on the highest human level), is *worshipping* someone. That kind of worship is different from conventional church worship. And it is the closest you will ever get to satisfaction as a human being. The consideration of Loving God must manifest as genuine experience with loving—not in otherworldly terms, but practically.

Loving God is an active process of considering what it is to Love God with "…thy whole heart and…soul and to love thy neighbor as thyself." (Mark 12:30-31.) In order to "love thy neighbor," you have to love yourself. Loving yourself has to do with humility and objectivity.

Your life in community is the testing ground, the laboratory. You must consider how you feel toward one another. If you felt loving toward one another, how would you act toward one another? It's very easy to act loving with a check-out girl at the supermarket who smiles all the time. You don't have to live with her. That is not relationship. The real consideration of relationship must take place with whom you live, and then it radiates outward. We are all nice when we are "out there"; there is no territory to defend. Relationship is a matter of who you live with.

We are all essentially loving individuals, but we don't express that because we have developed defense mechanisms against being hurt. We have all been hurt as children. A kid sees another kid being cruel to an animal and says, "Hey, stop it," and the kid gets beaten up because he was vulnerable. So we learn to protect ourselves against the hurt that conventionally comes to us when we are loving.

We don't love one another, not because we can't, but because we won't let ourselves. Every one of us has had a friend whom we really loved for a moment. If we were willing to admit that this moment actually happened, then we should wonder: "How can it be that way all the time?"

Loving someone is its own reward. It's ecstatic, free, full. You are bodily transported. I don't mean through sex. You can look at a baby from one hundred feet away and be bodily transported. Can you be that way with one another? If you love someone that freely your motives will probably be suspect—you will be misunderstood. You will be wide open and you are going to get hurt sometimes. But when the response is loving in return, it's worth it! Then there is an environment where people are really loving one another, not where people appear to be loving, like in a lot of spiritual communities you find today.

When people are loving with one another, the environment is one of delight, gentleness, bliss, ecstasy, rapture. Since you have to start somewhere, you start with how you treat people. If you can't do anything about "letting off steam," go scream outside...not to someone's face. The consideration of Loving God must begin with an active organic consideration of how we live with one another.

The more intimate you are with someone, the more important it is to start the consideration of Loving God within the context of that relationship. Freedom is what you love. Those of you who have ever been married know that the first thing you want to do is curtail your lover's freedom. You can't own another's freedom; if you do you will break that person.

So, treat one another as you would treat someone you love. That must be present as a disciplined commitment so that when they do something that really "gets your goat" you will still treat them as someone you love.

The only way you can do this is to objectively look at yourself at all times. If you are willing to look at who you are essentially then you will be able to treat each other lovingly. Then your life will turn around one hundred and eighty degrees. It will be full of enthusiasm and interest. That is the kind of community I would prefer to live in. The consideration of Loving God makes that available.

This consideration of Loving God is the highest possibility. This is the possibility wherein there can be boundless enthusiasm for spiritual Work. This is the possibility for real community.

AFTERWORD

About My Master

I could say many things about my Father, Yogi Ramsuratkumar, but as is often the case, the most sacred elements between a son and his Father must remain secrets of the heart. Still, there is much to reveal. Yogi Ramsuratkumar is a Beggar. He wears rags and lives amidst a massive collection of piles of every kind of "souvenir" from bags full of papers to overflowing dried flower malas. He is visited in these auspicious albeit unceremonious surroundings by a steady stream of devotees, all seeking His Blessings. One of the most striking aspects of His Presence (among a list too long to completely articulate) is His laughter. He is constantly laughing with the pure joy of spontaneous innocence, with the tones of the quality of a bubbling, gurgling brook, with the delight of a man both free of all attachment and, perhaps paradoxically, completely and irrevocably attached to Humankind. When He laughs, His eyes, those brilliant jewels of pure radiance, sparkle with the enjoyment of One whose care and concern for His children is absolute.

I met Yogi Ramsuratkumar physically almost 20 years ago but have known Him, or more accurately He has known me for eons. I think no one really ever finds Him but the appearance of finding Him is what defines being called, drawn like iron filings to a magnet by His unendingly flowing Love and Attraction. His Compassion is so overwhelming that when in His circle of gopis one can only rest in the complete comfort and sanctuary of His Benediction and His Grace.

He is not a Teacher, not a guru, neither a saint nor a sage and yet His universality embodies all of these and so much more. He calls Himself a dirty Sinner and a Madman. And so He is. He is, again paradoxically, just as we are. For aren't we all sinners and aren't we all a bit mad? But do not let this cause you to presume that you are like Him. Out of His boundless service to mankind He may be like us but He is so unique, so submitted to the Will of His Father in Heaven that we can only gasp in awe at such Magnificence, and should contemplate with wonder His singular Madness and His Blessed Sins.

Yogi Ramsuratkumar is my Father. In Him I put all my trust. He has broken my heart such that the cracks are the doorways through which God can enter at last. His demand is relentless and profound. It is a demand to see none but God, to assume none but God, to love and serve all. His demand is to drop the illusions of separation and find the Madness that His Father, Swami Papa Ramdas, gave to Him.

Yogi Ramsuratkumar, the God-child, Bhagawan, is the sole refuge of His true Devotees. He is my all, my Everything, my Hope. He is the Divine embodied, waiting, always waiting for His children. He is a heart-breaker yet who wouldn't yearn to have their heart shattered, melted by such a Love, such a Merciful One. This is heart-break that one prays for, that one treasures as the rarest of the rare of God's gifts to us, of His Graces.

Yogi Ramsuratkumar is my Father. May I be a son worthy of His Glance.

lee lozowick
Yogi Ramsuratkumar chei